Natural Nashville

Natural Nashville

A Guide to the Greenways and Nature Parks

Proceeds from the sale of this guide are used to
support the conservation and expansion of
Nashville's greenways and nature parks

ROBERT BRANDT

iUniverse LLC
Bloomington

Natural Nashville
A Guide to the Greenways and Nature Parks

iUniverse books may be ordered through booksellers or by contacting:

iUniverse LLC
1663 Liberty Drive
Bloomington, IN 47403
www.iuniverse.com
1-800-Authors (1-800-288-4677)

ISBN: 978-1-4759-6085-3 (sc)
ISBN: 978-1-4759-6086-0 (e)

Library of Congress Control Number: 2012922162

Printed in the United States of America

iUniverse rev. date: 11/18/2013

CONTENTS

IN MEMORY OF BOB BROWN

Bob Brown with Trouble at Beaman Park

Some people are geared more toward thinking. Some are geared more toward doing. Bob Brown was geared toward both. Anyone who enjoys the Tennessee outdoors can be grateful for that. Though Bob could always name someone who he claimed made a bigger contribution, the truth is that the modest, unassuming bank trust officer contributed more than anyone to the development of hiking trails in Tennessee.

Bob was a founder of the Tennessee Trails Association and the moving force behind the establishment of the Cumberland Trail, the linear state park that crosses the width of Tennessee from the Cumberland Gap to Chattanooga. He was involved in the passage of the 1971 Tennessee Scenic Trails Act. Bob was affiliated with Greenways for Nashville, the Nature Conservancy, the Tennessee Scenic Rivers Association, the Tennessee Parks and Greenways Foundation, and The Land Trust for Tennessee. He edited several editions of *Tennessee Trails*, a statewide hiking guide. He was a stalwart supporter of the Warner Parks.

Though he was educated as an engineer and worked in investments most of his life, Bob was a serious amateur historian and botanist. Anyone fortunate to walk in the woods with Bob discovered that there was hardly a plant he could not identify.

When Mayor Phil Bredesen determined to launch Nashville's greenways program, he turned to Bob Brown. Bob was involved in the planning and implementation of the greenways as well as the establishment of three large parks, Shelby Bottoms, Beaman, and Bells Bend.

Bob died in 2007. He left as his legacy many of the areas described in this guide.

GREENWAYS FOR NASHVILLE

Greenways for Nashville (GFN) is the non-profit coalition of individuals, groups, and businesses that supports the Metro Parks greenways program. GFN advocates for the preservation and protection of natural, scenic and cultural areas; the development of community recreational facilities; and the acquisition of land for preservation, greenways and related areas. The organization relies on volunteers. If you would like to contribute time, energy, or resources to help protect and expand Nashville's greenways, contact GFN at 615-862-8400 or at *www.greenwaysfornashville.org.*

PREFACE

"What's your favorite place?" People started asking me this after publication of *Touring the Middle Tennessee Backroads,* a book I wrote in 1995. My answer is always the same: "I like it all. If I didn't, it wouldn't be in the book. But what excites me the most is getting to know places close to home."

Nashville is my home. So the places that excite me the most are described in this new guide. Whether it's enjoying the wildflowers at the Warner Parks, hiking the ridges at Radnor Lake, walking through blooming Tennessee coneflowers at the Couchville Glade, bicycling at Shelby Bottoms and on the Stones River Greenway, or investigating the overlooked treasure of Mill Creek along its greenway segments, I love it all.

This guide results from the intersection of several of my interests: natural resource conservation, outdoor recreation, and writing. I am a life-long conservationist, most recently serving as vice-president of The Land Trust for Tennessee and as a member of the Greenways Commission under two mayors and as a board member of Greenways for Nashville.

I hiked and measured every trail in the region to write *Middle Tennessee on Foot.* I've floated the Harpeth River off and on for half a century. Though I cannot claim any expertise, I love to study our 400-plus species of blooming plants.

This makes the fifth book I've written on Tennessee outdoors and travel. In addition, my articles have appeared in *The Tennessee Conservationist, Tennessee Historical Quarterly, The Tennessean, Sierra,* and other periodicals.

I came up with the idea for this guide from a similar one, *Natural Bucks County: Guide to the Natural Areas,* covering a scenic and varied landscape outside Philadelphia. A frequent visitor there, I found it useful to have in one place all the information I needed to explore the county's considerable nature bounty. So I committed to writing one for Davidson County.

It's been difficult deciding when to publish this guide. Much of it was written more than ten years before publication. But we always have some great project on the horizon that should be included, so I kept putting it off. With the addition to the Warner Parks of the land north of Highway 100, I figured it was time get it out. Otherwise, it might never get published. It's a nice problem to have. And even as this guide comes out, there are several exciting projects in the works, some described in Appendix Three, which will make one of American's best networks of greenways and parks even better.

So stay in touch.

INTRODUCTION

The 533 square miles that make up Nashville and Davidson County—they have been one-in-the-same since 1963—embrace a natural environment of striking diversity. Elevations range from 375 feet on the Cumberland River to 1,160 feet atop the forested hills around Radnor Lake. There are places in the river bottoms where the soil is thirty feet deep, yet in the rocky cedar glades unique to this part of the world there are places with hardly any soil at all. The topography ranges from steep bluffs to level flood plains. There are patches of mature hardwood forest harboring huge trees, thick forests of evergreen cedars, fields that are being allowed to return to forest, desert-like areas where no trees can grow, and open meadows.

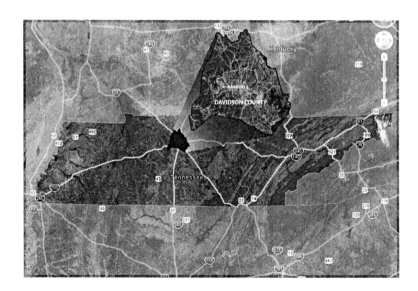

xvi | Robert Brandt

Much of this heterogeneous landscape has been preserved in an ever-expanding network of greenways and parks. Greenways are linear parks along stream corridors, and there are greenway segments along each of the seven major waterways in Davidson County. The larger parks offer opportunities to sample the distinct ecoregions that comprise Davidson County: Inner Central Basin, Outer Central Basin, and Western Highland Rim, as well as the Cumberland River corridor.

The greenways and parks are managed by several local, state, and federal entities. "Metro Parks" is shorthand for the parks department of Nashville's consolidated city-county government. *www.nashville.gov/parks/*. "State Parks" means the State Parks Division of the Tennessee Department of Environment and Conservation. *www.state.tn.us.environment/parks/*. The U. S. Army Corps of Engineers manages two areas on J. Percy Priest Lake and one at Old Hickory Dam. *www.lrn.usace.army.mil/op/jpp/rec/*. The National Park Service manages the Natchez Trace Parkway. *www.nps.gov/natr/*.

ONLINE UPDATES

Expansions of existing parks and greenways and establishment of new ones are ongoing. Annual updates of this guide are available at *www.greenwaysfornashville.org.*

ENJOYING THE GREENWAYS AND NATURE PARKS

ACTIVITIES

Greenways have **paved trails** suitable for walking, running, bicycling, in-line skating, baby strolling, and use by the disabled. Most of the parks have paved trails as well as **primitive trails** for hiking, ranging in length from short nature paths to trails of several miles.

Nashville Green Bikes offers **bicycles** that can be checked out seasonally at these locations on or near greenways: Antioch Community Center near the Mill Creek Greenway, Hartman Community Center near the Whites Creek Greenway, McCabe Community Center near the Richland Creek Greenway, Morgan Park Community Center and Riverfront Station near the Cumberland River Greenway, and the Shelby Bottoms Nature Center. Check availability of bikes at *www.nashvillebikeshare.org*.

Mountain biking on primitive trails is offered at Bells Bend, Hamilton Creek, Cane Ridge, and Percy Warner Parks and Long Hunter State Park. Biking is not allowed on hiking trails at any of the parks.

There are **bridle paths** in Peeler and Percy Warner Parks.

Camping by permit is allowed at Long Hunter State Park and Bells Bend Park.

Canoeing and kayaking are frequent activities on the Stones and Harpeth Rivers. Mill and Whites Creeks are floatable when the water level is not too low or too high. The Cumberland River, impounded as Cheatham Lake in Davidson

County, is more suitable for power boats, though it does receive some non-motorized boat use. **Sailing** is popular on J. Percy Priest Lake.

Birding is best around bodies of water. The Tennessee Wildlife Resources Agency and the National Audubon Society have teamed up to identify "Important Bird Areas" throughout Tennessee. Four of them are in Davidson County: Old Hickory Lake, Radnor Lake, Shelby Bottoms/Park, and the Warner Parks. Another, Cheatham Lake Wildlife Management Area, is just outside Nashville in neighboring Cheatham County.

Some type of plant is blooming in Nashville all year except in the dead of winter. The most popular places for **wildflowers** are the moist forests at Radnor Lake, Warner Parks, and Beaman Park and in the cedar glades at Long Hunter, Couchville Glade, Mount View Glade, and Anderson Road Recreation Area.

Fishing is popular on the Cumberland, Stones, and Harpeth Rivers and the large reservoirs. **Hunting** is not allowed in parks, but is allowed in adjoining Cheatham County not far from units of the Harpeth River State Park at the Cheatham Wildlife Management Area and on the Cumberland River at the Cheatham Lake Wildlife Management Area.

Naturalist-led activities are offered at Shelby Bottoms, Bells Bend, Long Hunter, Radnor Lake, Warner, and Beaman. Telephone inquires are welcome and schedules are usually available online (see "Nature Centers" below).

A variety of entities lead **organized outings**. The most active is the Nashville Hiking Meetup, an online-based group with thousands of members that organizes a dazzling array of outings and social events with something for all ages and every level of ability (*www.nashvillehiking.com*). Other groups sponsoring outings are the Tennessee Trails Association (*www.tennesseetrails. org*); the Tennessee Ornithological Society (*www.tnbirds.org*); the Tennessee Scenic Rivers Association (www.paddletsra.org); the Tennessee Native Plant Society (*www.tnps.org*); the Middle Tennessee Group of the Sierra Club (*www.tennessee.sierraclub.*

org); and the North American Butterfly Association (*www. nabamidtn.org*). Non-members are usually welcome.

NATURE CENTERS

The four largest Metro parks have intriguing nature centers that feature exhibits and activities, and the two large state parks have welcoming visitor centers with exhibits and activities. Nature centers at Shelby Bottoms, Bells Bend, and Beaman are registered as EarthCraft Certified. They were built using environmentally sensitive design and construction methods that minimize site impact, and they use natural lighting for public spaces and employ passive solar design.

Information about activities and events can be obtained directly from each park.

- **Beaman:** 5911 Old Hickory Boulevard, Ashland City, 37015; 615-862-8580; *www.nashville.gov/parks/ nature/bpnc.*
- **Bells Bend:** 4187 Old Hickory Boulevard, Nashville, 37218; 615-862-4187; *www.nashville.gov/parks/ nature/bbnc.*
- **Long Hunter:** 2910 Hobson Pike, Hermitage, 37076; 615-885-2422; *www.tn.gov/environment/parks/ LongHunter.*
- **Radnor Lake:** 1160 Otter Creek Road, Nashville, 37220; 615-373-3467; *www.tn.gov/environment/ parks/RadnorLake.*
- **Shelby Bottoms:** 1900 Davidson Street, Nashville, 37206; 615-862-8539; *www.nashville.gov/parks/ nature/sbnc.*
- **Warner:** 7311 Highway 100, Nashville, 37221; 615-352-6299; *www.nashville.gov/parks/wpnc.*

SAFETY

The lands and waters of Nashville's greenways and nature parks are generally benign. The biggest threat to visitors comes from their own carelessness. On the paved trails there is the potential for collisions between walkers and bicyclists and skaters. These trails are not intended for racing, so bicyclists and skaters should take care not to travel at speeds dangerous to others and should always obey the posted speed limit. Walkers should be alert for bicyclists and skaters.

Often the power of rushing water and the danger of cold water are not appreciated. Exercise caution when wading or floating, and stay out of streams and back up when streams are high. In the spring, water is often much colder than the air.

Creatures living in the woods pose little threat. There are poisonous snakes, but visitors rarely encounter them; just back away from a snake if you come upon one. Poison ivy is common in Nashville's woods.

Crime is rare on greenways and in the parks. The most common problem is car break-ins. Lock your car, and do not leave valuables exposed. It is best to put them out of sight before arriving at the trailhead, for at some trailheads car burglars have hidden so they can observe what is being put away.

NASHVILLE'S NATURAL LANDSCAPE

Geologists divide the earth into physiographic provinces and smaller physiographic regions. Tennessee is within five provinces and ten physiographic regions, making the Volunteer State the nation's most ecologically diverse non-coastal state. Nashville is in the middle of the state and is in two physiographic regions, the Nashville or Central Basin and the Western Highland Rim.

Under the guidance of the U.S. Environmental Protection Agency, these divisions have been refined into "ecoregions" of generally similar ecosystems that take into account not just geology and topography, but also vegetation, climate, soil, land use, wildlife, and hydrology. Nashville spreads over three ecoregions: the Inner Central Basin, the Outer Central Basin, and the Western Highland Rim. The Cumberland River creates its own environment as it weaves fifty-seven miles across the width of Davidson County in nine giant bends. A good case could be made that the river corridor is its own ecoregion.

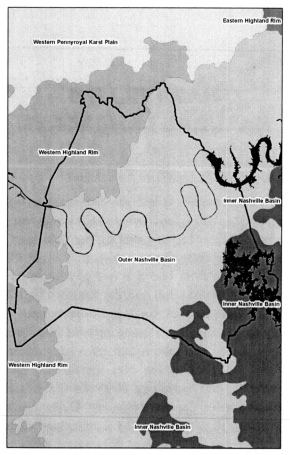

Ecoregions of Davidson County

The properties and quality of the soil have much to do with what grows where, and Davidson County is home to no fewer than ten different soil types.

Topography—the lay and slope of the land—plays a major role in the natural environment, for it determines how much sunlight a given area receives, and the amount of sunlight helps determine the characteristics of the plant life. With so many steep hills facing all directions, Nashville's natural environment is characterized by extremes. The ecosystems on the north slopes of some ridges are so different from those on the south of the same ridges, they do not seem like they are in the same place.

Though enormous progress has been made in restoring Nashville's natural environment from sometimes thoughtless human activity, a few seemingly intractable problems continue. Forest fragmentation, the invasion of non-native or "exotic" plants, suburban sprawl, and pollution all have the effect of reducing the number of plants and animals. This causes a reduction in biological diversity or "biodiversity." Continued reduction in biodiversity eventually leads to species extinction.

NASHVILLE'S FORESTS

The early explorers, hunters, and pioneers who came into the uninhabited Cumberland country in the 1700s found a lush primeval forest broken only occasionally by marshes, river bluffs, and grassy or rocky forest openings. That primeval forest was part of the larger deciduous forest that once spread over much of the eastern United States. (The term "deciduous" means summer green, trees that shed their leaves in winter, as opposed to evergreens that stay green year-round.) Accounts of the earliest settlers report tulip poplar trees six or seven feet in diameter, as well as an abundance of enormous black walnut, hickory, maple, oak, beech and elm. To the southeast the pioneers discovered evergreen cedar forests. Forest cover, then, is the natural condition of nearly all Davidson County. If lawns, farm fields, and golf courses were left alone, most of them would revert to forest.

Because of the wide variety of soil and topography, the forest plants growing in Nashville's natural areas are quite varied as well. This diversity is enhanced even more because Nashville is in a transition zone among forest types. The city is in the *western mesophytic* forest region that extends westward from the Cumberland Plateau, the western-most edge of the Appalachian Mountains rising eighty or so miles east of Nashville. ("Mesophytic" means requiring a medium amount of moisture.) The Plateau is in the *mixed mesophytic* forest region. But the border of the mixed mesophytic region tends to be irregular, and the change from it to the western mesophytic region is gradual.

Visitors encounter four or five kinds of forest habitat in the parks of Nashville-Davidson County. In the Outer Central Basin on the north-facing slopes of the Harpeth Hills and on the Western Highland Rim, big trees populate cooler moist areas, giving the coves and hollows at Beaman Park, Radnor Lake, and the Warner Parks the feel of a forest in the Appalachian Mountains. Common trees are sugar maple, bitternut hickory, shagbark hickory, beech, tulip poplar, white oak, red oak, and basswood. Mountain laurel grows on some of the ridges, as does wild azalea.

On the Outer Central Basin's south-facing slopes where it is drier and the soil is often rockier, common trees are chinquapin oak, black oak, hackberry, pignut hickory, and cedar. The forest of the Inner Basin is similar, though in places there are pure stands of cedar.

Along the banks of the Cumberland River and its major tributaries the tree canopy is made up of silver maple, boxelder, sycamore, and cottonwood, and in the adjacent moist bottoms there is red maple, pin oak, sweetgum, and several species of elm.

There are places where not many trees grow, even in their natural state. The marshes along the rivers are like that. While they may have a scattering of cottonwood, willow, and sycamore, more common are smaller plants such as buttonbush, swamp mallow, sedges, and swamp milkweed. Up on the Western Highland Rim, outcroppings of shale and siltstone create "barrens" covered in grass with a few post oaks and cedars here and there. These areas are found at Beaman Park.

The cedar glades of the Inner Central Basin have hardly any trees at all (see p. 14). They get their name "cedar" because they are in cedar forests. Some glades are littered with broken rocks while others are covered in grass.

THE FOREST AS A COMMUNITY

A forest is more than a collection of trees; it is a complex interconnecting network of organisms, often described as an "ecosystem." The word "system" means the same in the forest as it does elsewhere, such as a railroad or an airline. Everything is interconnected. A hospital is a good example; a multitude of different functions and personnel work together to provide services. There are buildings, nurses, doctors, labs, admissions, housekeeping, and so on. The same is true for the forest. In addition to trees, forests have water, soil, birds, mammals, reptiles, amphibians, insects, fungi, and, of course, people. In ideal conditions they all work in harmony, each relying on the other for survival. The forest can become unhealthy when these interdependent relationships are interrupted.

FOREST SUCCESSION

The process by which a disturbed forest returns to its original state is called "succession." If continued land-clearing stops, a natural succession from forbs-to-shrubs-to-young forest-to-mature forest-to-climax forest will follow. A climax forest is one in which succession is complete and the forest has changed all it is going to change, a process that takes fifty to one hundred years depending on the conditions.

Permanent European and African-American settlement of Nashville and Middle Tennessee dates to 1779-80 and the "great leap westward" as Tennessee's state historian Walter Durham tagged it. Led by James Robertson (1742-1814) and John Donelson (1718-1785), hundreds of men, women, and children made perilous land and water journeys through the wilderness from present-day Upper East Tennessee. As settlement spread out from the river, much of the land was cleared for building and agriculture, and trees were harvested from the remaining forest.

Nashville became an important Union army supply depot and garrison early in the Civil War and remained so for more than three years. Still more trees were harvested to satisfy the insatiable need for wood for buildings, fortifications and fuel. Photographs from the war years show vast denuded landscapes. Over time, and particularly on protected public land, the forests grew back through succession.

This phenomenon of forest succession can be observed in Nashville's larger preserves where portions of formerly open land are no longer kept cleared. The forest around the Radnor Lake visitor center, for example, was open field as late as the 1970s. The former cropland at Shelby Bottoms being allowed to revert to forest was kept cleared as late as the 1990s. The same is true at Bells Bend Park. These places look a little different each year, and if left alone they will eventually reach climax.

In two of the largest parks, Radnor Lake and the Warner Parks, it has been a long time—going on a century in some spots—since there has been any significant logging, and there are patches of climax or near-climax forest. Shelby Bottoms has some patches of very old forest as well. At Beaman Park, stumps from logging are visible, but they will decompose over time as the forest grows toward climax. Most of Nashville's private forest continues to have trees harvested, and so long as that continues, the succession will never reach climax.

The term "old growth" describes a forest in which there is no evidence that trees have ever been harvested. Old growth is rare in the eastern United States. Well-known samples in Tennessee are in the Savage Gulf State Natural Area on the Cumberland Plateau and in the Great Smoky Mountains National Park. There is one patch of old growth forest in Nashville, on the former Hill Tract between Highway 100 and US 70S that is now part of the Warner Parks. The trees there are enormous.

Climax forest in other parts of Nashville's parks is or will be largely indistinguishable from old growth.

FOREST FRAGMENTATION

The interruption of a continuous forest by clearing leads to "forest fragmentation." Some species of plants and animals thrive deep in the forest interior while others thrive on the forest edge. ("Forest interior" is defined as the portion a thousand feet or so from the edge.) If a forest fragment is so small that little or any of it is that deep, then interior species, particularly the animals that need a deep forest, cannot survive. That is one reason bears no longer live in Nashville.

The phenomena of fragmentation can be observed at Shelby Bottoms where only patches of woods remain. Box turtles, wood frogs, and such birds as the red-shouldered hawk, pileated woodpecker, and many species of songbirds do not thrive like they once did due to fragmentation.

Cowbirds pose a particular problem. These edge-loving blackbirds lay their eggs—often as many as forty to fifty over the course of a breeding season—in the nests of other species. With no deep forest to protect them, birds that nest in the forest interior are more vulnerable to having their nests taken over by these "nest parasites," thus reducing the population of birds that nest in the interior of the forest. Other animals that thrive on the forest edge are deer, raccoon, and opossum. Birds such as grackles, cardinals, and blue jays like the edges.

EXOTIC PLANTS

The term "exotic" refers to plants that are not native to the region but that have been introduced as ornamentals, as highway plantings, or for erosion control. They are sometimes referred to as "invasive" plants. Many exotics rapidly grow to maturity, have prolific reproduction, and have highly successful seed dispersal. They lack natural predators, competitors, and climatic conditions that would keep their numbers in check and often spread rampantly, out-competing the native plants.

Kudzu is the exotic most people in the South know about. This climbing vine was introduced from Japan in the 1930s to control erosion—a task it does not perform well—and takes over everything in its path, even giant oak trees. It is practically impossible to eradicate. After years of trying to remove kudzu at Radnor Lake by cutting it back, and fearful of using potentially harmful herbicides, park management was finally able to rid the natural area of kudzu by turning goats loose in the infested spots.

Bush honeysuckle is another troublesome exotic. It keeps its green leaves well into winter, and often leafs out in the spring before the wildflowers, depriving them of the sunlight they need. These pesky plants are perverse inside the Belle Meade Boulevard entrance to Percy Warner Park and in many other areas of the park. Physical removal is one way to reduce their population, and each fall volunteers descend on the Warner Parks and Radnor to remove as many these invasive plants as possible.

Common privet was introduced as a hedge plant and takes over wherever it grows. It clogs moist areas at Shelby Bottoms, the Warner Parks, and along the Stones River and Richland Creek Greenways.

The exotic creeping euonymus, or winter creeper, has gotten loose in the forest, creating a monoculture that prevents the growth of native wildflowers. There are places at Long Hunter State Park and the Warner Parks where the ground is carpeted with the plant.

Fortunately, Beaman Park has escaped the exotic invasion. That is one reason plans for bridle paths were scrapped, for seeds of invasive plants are often spread in horse droppings.

Landowners can reduce the influx of destructive exotics by using native plants in landscaping. The Warner Parks Nature Center provides helpful information, including the location of local nurseries that specialize in native plants.

CEDAR GLADES

Cedar glades are the most distinctive ecological feature of Middle Tennessee's Inner Central Basin. The glades are rocky openings in the cedar forest where the soil is too shallow for trees to take root, and are covered with colorful wildflowers during the growing season.

Summer surface temperatures are often ten to thirty degrees hotter than in the adjacent woods, making the dry glades mini-deserts. Prickly pear cactus and yucca grow in the glades, as do some 350 other plants that have adapted to the harsh environment. The glades are unique to Middle Tennessee and are home to more than twenty plant species that are not found anywhere else on earth. Two of them, Pyne's ground plumb and leafy prairie-clover, are on the endangered species list. The Tennessee coneflower was once listed as endangered, but has made a comeback and was "delisted" in 2011.

This rocky habitat is suitable for several reptiles, including the fence lizard, southeastern crowned snake, eastern milk snake, and five-linked skink. Birds associated with the open glades include the killdeer, common nighthawk, prairie warbler, yellow-breasted chat, rufous sided towhee, indigo bunting, white-eyed vireo, field sparrow, and lark sparrow. The cedar glades are the most reliable places in the region to see butterflies such as the southern dogface and goatweed leafwing.

Because crops cannot grow in the rocky glades, they were considered wasteland and used for dumping. The first scientist to appreciate their uniqueness was Dr. Augustin Gattinger, whose book *Flora of Tennessee* was published in 1901. But it was Vanderbilt University botanist Elsie Quarterman, who, in modern times stimulated interest in the glades. Starting with her dissertation as a Duke University graduate student in 1948 and continuing through the balance of the twentieth century, Dr. Quarterman studied the glades and popularized interest in them. In 1968, at the Mount View Glade, she discovered Tennessee coneflowers, a species thought to be extinct. There are now thirty-five colonies of the tall flower.

Thanks to the aggressive conservation effort of The Nature Conservancy and the Tennessee Department of Environment and Conservation, many cedar glades are protected as officially designated state natural areas, including one glade named for Dr. Quarterman. In Davidson County, Long Hunter State Park, Couchville Glade, Mount View Glade, and Anderson Road Recreation Area have nice samples of cedar glades, as do protected areas in adjacent Rutherford and Wilson Counties. For a complete list of state natural areas, check *www.tn.gov/environment/na/natareas/*

Middle Tennessee State University is home to the Center for Cedar Glade Studies where more information about the glades is available, including about programs and field trips. *www.mtsu.edu/~gladectr.*

GREENWAYS
AND
NATURE PARKS

ALONG THE CUMBERLAND RIVER

The Cumberland River meanders for fifty-five graceful miles from east to west through Nashville-Davidson County in nine giant bends that slice the county roughly in half. The remnant bottomland forest and deep rich soils of the floodplain create an environment unlike any other in Nashville. Common trees along the banks include silver maple, boxelder, sycamore, and cottonwood. The adjoining bottoms include elm, ash, red maple, sweetgum, and pin oak. Though upstream dams control the flow of the river through Nashville, the river does get high enough now and then to create a few wetland habitats.

The absence of bridges at the ends of two of the big bends, Neelys to the east and Bells to the west, has kept them isolated islands of rural tranquility. There are large nature parks in both bends, and there are greenway segments along other parts of the Cumberland River as well.

The Cumberland starts as a trickle deep in the mountains of Eastern Kentucky. Along its 700-mile length, the river dips into Tennessee for a 300-mile run before returning to the Bluegrass State to give its waters to the mighty Ohio River near Paducah not far from the mouth of the larger Tennessee River. By the time the Cumberland River reaches Nashville, it has received the waters of several major tributaries: the Big South Fork, the Obey-Wolf River system, the Roaring River, and the Caney Fork. The Stones River empties into the Cumberland in Nashville, and the Harpeth does the same just downstream. The Red River flows into the Cumberland farther downstream at Clarksville.

Though Cheatham Dam impounds the Cumberland through Nashville, the river stays within its natural bed, retaining its character as a river. Its width through Davidson County averages around 350 feet. Closer to the dam in Cheatham County there are some sloughs that offer excellent viewing of migratory waterfowl, shorebirds, and other animals such as muskrat, beaver, and an occasional otter.

The name "Cumberland" has been given to countless mountains, rivers, streams, towns, and counties in Tennessee and Kentucky. They all derive from the same source. Dr. Thomas Walker of Virginia was exploring beyond the fringe of colonial America in 1748 when he came upon the sheer mountain escarpment that hems in on the west the Great Appalachian Valley. He named the range in honor of the English Prince William Augustus, the Duke of Cumberland, son of King George II. Walker gave the name to the gap that offers passage through the sheer green wall and to the small river he found west of the gap.

The Cumberland River has historically been divided into three parts. "Lower Cumberland" is the name applied to the river downstream from Nashville. "Upper Cumberland" has meant the river from Nashville upstream to what was the head of navigation, Burnside, Kentucky. The third part from Burnside to the source was never navigable. Steamboat traffic on the Cumberland River was important to the growth of Nashville from the time the first steamboat reached the city in 1819 until the railroads began to proliferate a half-century later. No railroad penetrated the rugged Upper Cumberland region for a long time, so steamboat traffic continued to be important there into the first two decades of the twentieth century. That is how Captain Tom Ryman, the builder of what came to be called the Ryman Auditorium, made his fortune, in the Upper Cumberland steamboat trade. The Cumberland today is an important waterway for barge traffic.

The Metro Parks greenways master plan calls for greenway segments along the river's entire length in Davidson County.

Nashville's local government has launched an ambitious downtown riverfront development that will change the character of the area and make the Cumberland more accessible. Plans call for an urban forest, wetlands, docks, fountains, an amphitheater, picnic areas, and more walkways. As of this writing, Cumberland Park is open on the east bank between the Shelby Street and the Korean Veterans Memorial Bridges.

OLD HICKORY NATURE TRAIL

Brief Description: *Forest and wetland*
Location: *Old Hickory: off Old Hickory Boulevard (TN 45) near the end of the dam*
Facilities: *Paved trail, hiking trail, wildlife observation site, boat ramp nearby, restrooms at nearby beach area*
Management: *Corps of Engineers*

Area Description

This tiny preserve in Hadley Bend near Old Hickory Dam consists of three walking loops denominated "Woodland," "Willow Swamp," and "Wildlife," and a paved trail on an old railroad grade connecting the loops, all totaling 1.5 miles in length. The area includes a thicket of tall loblolly pines that were planted in 1967. (Pines are not native to this part of Tennessee.) Native trees in this area are those that thrive in wetlands—cottonwood, willow, and sycamore. Mammals that inhabit this spot include groundhog (woodchuck), raccoon, squirrel, rabbit, and possum.

The Corps of Engineers in the early 1950s constructed Old Hickory Dam twenty-five miles upstream from downtown Nashville, creating a lake with 440 miles of shoreline. Unlike at nearby J. Percy Priest Lake, where most of the surrounding land is protected in public ownership, suburban development on Old Hickory Lake reaches right to the water's edge. Nevertheless, the lake has attracted a wide variety of birds and includes the largest breeding colonies of wading birds in Middle Tennessee's Central Basin. Old Hickory Lake has been designated an "Important Bird Area" by the Tennessee Wildlife Resources Agency and National Audubon Society. Wading birds spotted around the lake include black-crowned night heron, great blue heron, great egret, and double-crested cormorant. Ospreys can occasionally be seen circling over the lake casting an eye for unsuspecting fish. There are in addition a multitude of winter waterfowl—ducks, geese, loons, grebes, gulls, terns, and swallows.

"Old Hickory" was the nickname given to Andrew Jackson (1767-1845), seventh President of the United States. His home, The Hermitage, is nearby. The village of Old Hickory traces its origins to the DuPont gunpowder plant started in 1918 during World War I. The planned village built for the workers contained more than 500 residences, many of which still stand. The plant later switched to making rayon.

Peeler Park

Brief description: Cumberland River bank, forest, fields, and wetland
Location: Madison: off Neelys Bend Road and Menees Lane
Facilities: Paved trail, hiking trails, bridle paths, boat ramp
Management: Metro Parks

Area Description

Peeler Park's 659 acres take in the southeastern tip of Neelys Bend, one of the least developed of Nashville's nine Cumberland River bends. The park has become a popular place for Madison-area residents to enjoy the outdoors, and it is a great place to observe a landscape transitioning back to its natural state. Before Metro Parks acquired the original Peeler Park land in 1963, the farm of the Euston N. Peeler family consisted of pasture and cropland, as well as some clumps of woods and the tree-lined riverbank. The forest is slowly reclaiming some of the former farmland through "forest succession" (see p. 10).

A 2.7-mile paved greenway trail with a loop at the end runs through Peeler's old fields, along the Cumberland River bank, and across a soggy woodland. This seasonal wetland that is home to some large ash trees is crossed on a boardwalk built with funds provided by the Memorial Foundation. Other parts of the older woods have a variety of oak as well as elm, shellbark hickory, and red maple. The riverbank is lined with cottonwood, sycamore, and silver maple.

Peeler is one of two Nashville parks with bridle paths

There is a heron rookery at Peeler Park where water-loving great blue heron hatch their young. The park is also home to kingfisher and several kinds of woodpecker, plus mammals common in Middle Tennessee such as deer and raccoon. Wild turkey is abundant, and pairs of bald eagles have been spotted at Peeler.

Under the leadership of Mayor Karl Dean, Metro Parks in 2009 acquired the adjoining 388-acre Taylor Farm to add to the existing 271-acre Peeler Park, thus more than doubling its size. The Taylor Farm is made up of 100 acres of wetlands and floodplain and 288 acres of rolling upland fields and woodlands. Facilities in the Taylor addition will include paved trails, hiking trails, and bridle paths connecting to the existing Peeler Park trails.

The big bend is named for William Neely, one of Davidson County's original settlers who arrived with the James Robertson party in December 1779. Neely was killed in the bend in an Indian attack the following year, and the bend has borne his name ever since.

Peeler Park: A Poem
Jim Forkum

Up from bed I hit the floor
A new day soon begins
Anticipation fills the air
Until the new day ends.

I find my way to Peeler Park
My anticipation builds
As I walk up to the trailhead
Light begins to find the fields.

My path is along the Cumberland
The trail laid out for me
But sometimes I ease off the path
Just to see what I can see.

It is the perfect time
That I should venture here
To hear the turkey as they fly down
To glimpse the fox or deer.

I come not minding weather
Regardless warm or cold
It may even rain or snow
And the wind is ever bold.

I come here for the solitude
It puts my mind at ease
It is a special place indeed
Where there is a certain peace.

I see the great blue herons nest
And where the beaver cut his trees
There are so many other things
To see down on my knees.

If things are worth preserving
For the eagle and meadowlark
Come see the place that God made
Come see our Peeler Park.

Come and see the wonders
But leave it as you came
A special place resides there
Amongst the creatures in the cane.

Jim Forkum represented the Neelys Bend area in the Metro Council.

SHELBY BOTTOMS GREENWAY AND NATURE PARK

Brief Description: Cumberland River bank, bottomland hardwood
forest, fields, and wetlands
Location: East Nashville and Inglewood
Facilities: Paved trail, hiking trails, wildlife observation sites, boat
ramp nearby, nature center, restrooms
Management: Metro Parks

Area Description

This 945-acre crescent-shaped preserve a stone's throw
from downtown Nashville protects three-and-one-half miles of
the Cumberland River bank and a rare remnant of river bottom
habitat. Since it opened to the public in the mid-1990s, Shelby
Bottoms has become one of Metro Parks most popular units.
Visitors come from all over to enjoy a wide variety of habitats
and a stunning diversity of wildlife—birds, in particular—on a
network of more than six miles of paved trails and a like length
of primitive trails.

The paved trail covers the preserve from end-to-end. There
are loops at each end of it, and paved extensions linking the
trail to parking areas and neighborhood access points in East
Nashville and Inglewood. The paved trail stays fairly close to
the river, while the primitive trails are inland.

Shelby Bottoms

The Davidson Street Connector, a section of the Music City Bikeway (see p. 69), extends 2.75 miles from Shelby Bottoms through Shelby Park and on to the Shelby Street Bridge and a connection with the Cumberland River Greenway downtown.

The popularity of Shelby Bottoms was enhanced in 2008 with the opening of the pedestrian bridge spanning the Cumberland River connecting Shelby Bottoms to the Stones River Greenway at Two Rivers Park in Pennington Bend (see p. 28). Residents of Donelson who drove for miles to Shelby Bottoms can now get there with a short walk across the bridge. From the Shelby Bottoms Nature Center to the J. Percy Priest Dam, the continuous length of paved trail is about twelve miles. This is the final leg of the Music City Bikeway.

Cumberland River Pedestrian Bridge

The Cumberland River Pedestrian Bridge links Shelby Bottoms in East Nashville and Inglewood to the Stones River Greenway in Donelson. Completed in 2008, the suspension bridge is designed to resemble the original Woodland Street Bridge that once connected downtown to Edgefield, today's East Nashville. The pedestrian bridge is 700 feet long and 80 feet above river. The Tennessee Department of Transportation provided part of the funding and insured that there is a tunnel under Briley Parkway to carry the greenway to the bridge from Two Rivers Park. The Tennessee Wildlife Resources Agency awarded Metro Parks a grant to build the shorebird pond on the Shelby Bottoms side in the area where soil was taken to build the mound that allows visitors to circle up to the East Nashville end of the bridge. This is an excellent spot to bird watch. The views from the bridge are spectacular, giving viewers vistas of the Cumberland River and the surrounding bluffs and bottoms.

Shelby Bottoms is not pristine wilderness. Shortly after they arrived in 1779-80, the earliest settlers cut timber for housing and other uses and cleared land for farming. They drained the wetlands as well. But unlike much of the rest of Davidson County, nothing substantial was ever built in the bottoms because of flooding. Row crops were grown in the bottoms right up to 1991 when Metro Parks acquired the area. The result of this human alteration of the landscape is an ecosystem fragmented into several parts. While the fragmentation is regrettable in some respects—the opportunity to enjoy and study an unaltered river bottom environment is lost, and animals that require more uninterrupted forest can no longer survive there (see p. 12)—it is desirable in another respect. The several distinct parts of Shelby Bottoms provide a variety of habitats. There is the riverbank shaded by large silver maple, boxelder, sycamore, cottonwood, basswood, and, in the understory, red maple. Cane once was abundant in the bottoms, and a little of it is still left, though it tends to be overtaken by the non-native or "exotic" privet and bush honeysuckle that plague most of Nashville's parks.

The marshes are another habitat at Shelby Bottoms. In the marshes' more open parts grow sedges, swamp milkweed, cardinal flower, and monkey flower. Along the edge grow blue beech and cane. The woods around the marshes are inhabited by cottonwood, black willow, sycamore, and green ash. The buttonbush that attracts butterflies during its summer bloom is a common shrub around the marshes. In the moist ravines or draws leading to the river, such native species as boxelder, honey locust, hackberry, walnut, cane, and spicebush compete with non-native species. Only a slight rise in elevation makes a big difference in the bottoms' environment. In the forest away from the river, expect to find several kinds of oak—shumard, white, red, and burr—along with several kinds of hickory—shagbark, red pignut, mockernut, and pignut. Hackberry and elm live there too, and when the land dips toward the marshes, there are elm, green ash, silver maple, red maple, pin oak, and sweetgum.

It has been a while since trees were cut in Shelby Bottoms, so there are some really big ones growing in the rich moist soil. There are Tennessee's largest basswood, Carolina hickory, green hawthorn, swamp privet, and shellbark hickory. There are also Davidson County's largest swamp chestnut oak, silver maple, shagbark hickory, and sweet gum. A shingle oak at Shelby Bottoms is tied for the largest in the United States.

With its wide variety of habitats, Shelby Bottoms was a popular place for birding long before Metro Parks acquired it, and it has only gotten better with public access. Several ponds and other wetlands have been constructed and observation platforms are strategically placed throughout the 945 acres.

These wetlands provide shorebirds, waders, and other waterfowl a resting place during migration. The Tennessee Ornithological Society website lists 217 bird species that have been observed at Shelby Bottoms and adjacent Shelby Park (*www.tn.birds.org*).

Shelby Bottoms

This part of East Nashville is identified with the Fort family that once owned the land and with its most famous member, Cornelia Fort (1919-1943). Not long after her 1939 graduation from Sarah Lawrence College in New York and acceptance into the Junior League in Nashville, she turned to aviation. She was actually in the air giving flying lessons near Pearl Harbor when the Japanese attacked on December 7, 1941. Fort became one of twenty-eight women who started the Women's Auxiliary Ferrying Squadron or "WAFS." These pioneering aviators took on the task of ferrying military aircraft from the factories to the airfields. While on a mission on March 21, 1943, Cornelia Fort became a World War II casualty when she was killed in a mid-air collision, the first ever American woman pilot to die in the line of duty.

The story of this remarkable woman accounts for why the small private airport just outside the park boundary was named the Cornelia Fort Airpark. Following damage in the May 2010 floods, and with assistance from Cornelia Fort's family, Metro Parks acquired 135 acres that included the small airport and incorporated them into the nature park.

Both the greenway and adjacent Shelby Park are named for Dr. John Shelby, who once owned the land.

Natural Rhythms at Shelby Bottoms
Carter Harkins

The urban life has its pleasures and benefits, to be sure. But there are days when a soul longs to step away, to escape the constant, pulsing activity of the city, to find a green and quiet place in which to relish its own company. For me, that place has been Shelby Bottoms.

Over the years I have explored many miles of its paved and mowed hiking trails. There are views along the river that, despite the close proximity to the industrial area of downtown, still manage to keep me lingering for a glimpse of the golden sun playing against the old abandoned bridge tower, as it reflects in the still waters of the opposite bank.

Farther along the trail is a wooden bridge that spans a bog. During the warmer and wetter spring months, this bog can play host to hundreds of croaking bullfrogs, all comfortably nestled in hiding places under the boughs of just-budding trees, happy to join in the noisy chorus which welcomes in the new growing season once again. This is a different kind of cacophony, this ebbing and flowing of the natural world, and unlike the adjacent urban neighborhood in which I live, here I can still hear myself think.

For much the same reasons as my own, I suspect, birds are especially interested in this park, and I can always find a few of my favorite winged denizens among the berry-laden branches and thickets that line the trails. The bursts of blue color that flash across the trails in April, as jays and warblers pursue love, is one of the most welcome harbingers of spring. Even the occasional mockingbird, blessing the trail with his best cell-phone imitation, cannot stir any impulse in me above an amused smirk, as I reflect on the reality that it is the very world I have temporarily disconnected from which now supplies this excellent impersonator with his material. I cannot help but wonder if he intends to convey a deeper meaning through that which he mocks. I search the trees with my binoculars, looking for the hurler of such poignant accusations, but cannot find him.

Most of the time, though, my binoculars are trained much lower, focusing along the edges of the grassy trails, hoping to spot eastern-tailed blues, spring azures, and falcate orangetips flitting from red clover blooms to honeysuckle blossoms. Butterflies are my muse on this May afternoon, and after a cold winter indoors, my heart skips along with them, as together we celebrate the sun and its warmth, and the freedom it brings to our rejuvenated souls.

The fall of the year will bring the Monarchs, those kingly gliders of the skies. Among fields overtaken with black-eyed Susans and orange, flowery milkweed, one can find hundreds at a time, canvassing the heads of flowers in their courtly dance. There will be times in February when my body will ache to know that sight again. But for now, in this moment, I am content. It is here I can even almost forget what it is to live the urban life.

Carter Harkins lives in East Nashville with his wife and son and is owner of Harkins Creative.

SHELBY PARK

Brief Description: Developed Park with a natural area in its northern extremity
Location: East Nashville
Facilities: Hiking trail, boat ramp, restrooms
Management: Metro Parks

Area Description

With the expanse of the bigger and wilder Shelby Bottoms next to it, it is easy to overlook the natural features of the greenway's older and more developed partner, 361-acre Shelby Park. Though much of the park is developed for sports, there are some relatively undeveloped parts in the rugged landscape along the park's northern extremity. The two loop trails of .7 and 1.8 miles that take off from the trailhead by the community center on South 20th Street offer a nice opportunity to wander through an urban forest.

There are some unbelievably tall, matchstick-straight trees particularly along the abandoned road near the park's eastern boundary. Common species include several oak (burr, red, chinquapin, white, pin, shingle, shumard) as well as shellbark and bitternut hickory, sugar maple, beech, tulip poplar, and elm. Willow and sycamore congregate around the lake and creeks that feed it. There is one area populated by non-native evergreens: white pine, Norway spruce, and white fir. Wildflowers are not as abundant as in the less developed parks, but they are there, with a nice sample of spring beauty, May apple, and phlox in the spring.

An interesting feature of Shelby Park is the stream that emerges from a cave before tumbling down the hill.

While year-round bird watching takes place in the nearby bottoms, birders tend to use Shelby Park more during spring and fall seasonal migrations when a cacophony of bird songs competes with the sounds of urban living. Several warblers visit in the spring, and fall brings olive-sided flycatchers and orioles as well as other species. Waterfowl are regulars at the lake. Even the ball fields have their share of birds, as some red-tailed hawks have nested around them.

Owls

Three species of owls common in Nashville are the barred owl, the eastern screech owl, and the great horned owl. The screech owl is the smallest, often no bigger than a common robin or cardinal. The great horned owl is the biggest, a large creature with a broad wingspan that enables it to fly noiselessly through woods in search of prey. Seeing an owl may take some stealth. They are not overly fond of people, are well disguised by their color, and are often high up in trees. Owls are mostly nocturnal, so dawn and dusk are the best times to catch a glimpse of one. Hearing an owl is a different matter. The most familiar call is that of the barred owl, the hoots that give it the alternative name of "hoot owl." As its name suggests, the screech owl screeches. The great horned owl has a series of three to five low hoots.

The Owl Hollow Trail in Edwin Warner Park is a good place to look for owls.

Shelby has been a public park since 1912 when the City of Nashville purchased the land from a bankrupt amusement park. The little lake circled by the trails is named for John Sevier (1745-1815), Tennessee's governor when the state was admitted to the Union in 1796, and before that, governor of "The Lost State of Franklin," the failed attempt in the 1780s to create a new state in East Tennessee.

CUMBERLAND RIVER GREENWAY: EAST BANK, DOWNTOWN, AND NORTH NASHVILLE

Brief description: Paved trail and sidewalks in highly urbanized area, public art, historic sites
Location: Downtown, East Nashville, and North Nashville
Facilities: Paved trails, restrooms at the Bridge Building, Riverfront Park, and Farmers Market
Management: Metro Parks

Area Description

These greenway segments on opposite banks of the Cumberland River provide nice places to walk in the heart of town. Despite the urban setting, the river's natural features are still in evidence, and the greenway visits historic sites and some fascinating installations of public art. The greenway on the west or downtown side of the river stretches downstream through North Nashville to connect with the MetroCenter Levee segment of the Cumberland River Greenway.

The implementation of plans to remake the Cumberland River bank on both sides of the river will likely alter the existing greenway pattern, and there are plans to extend the greenway upstream on the west or downtown bank of the river. Cumberland Park opened in 2012 on the east bank between the Shelby Street and Korean Veterans Memorial Bridges. It is a magnificent area with a riverfront promenade that links up with the East Bank Greenway, as well as an amphitheater and several inviting children's play areas that include a fountain.

A nice loop walk of a half-hour to hour is to combine the East Bank Greenway with Riverfront Park, a short stretch of the Cumberland River Greenway, and river crossings on the historic pedestrian-only Shelby Street Bridge and the sidewalk on the Woodland Street Bridge.

The East Bank Greenway runs between the river and LP Field, since 1999 the 69,000-seat home of the Tennessee Titans of the National Football League. The greenway leads to the East Nashville end of the beautiful Shelby Street Bridge. Adorned with art and comfortable places to sit, the iron truss bridge dates to 1909 and was converted to a pedestrian bridge in 2003. It is on the National Register of Historic Places. Near the bridge on the site of a once-thriving barge construction business stand the twisted pieces of red steel that form Ghost Ballet for the East Bank Machine Works, sculpture by Alice Aycock.

The east end of the bridge is the start of the Davidson Street Bicycle Connector, a segment of the Music City Bikeway that runs along Davidson Street for 2.73 miles to Shelby Bottoms.

The Shelby Street Bridge touches ground on the west bank by the Schermerhorn Symphony Center, one of America's great music halls. The return to the river from the end of the bridge leads to Riverfront Park.

The Cumberland River Greenway picks up at the downstream end of Riverfront Park at First Avenue North and Church Street, just beyond sculptor Puryear Mims' 1962 statues of the 1780 reunion of James Robertson and John Donelson commemorating the beginning of Nashville near this spot.

The greenway veers off from First Avenue North on the sidewalk along the Gay Street Connector and soon passes Alan LeQuire's imposing statue of Timothy Demonbreun (1747-1826), the French-Canadian fur trader who arrived in these parts around 1769 and settled in Nashville for good in 1790. For walking the loop, pass under the first bridge and climb the stairs to the Public Square in front of the New Deal-era Courthouse and re-cross the river on the Woodland Street Bridge.

The greenway continues downstream atop the river bluffs next to the Justice A. A. Birch Building and passes under the busy railroad tracks at the end of the bridge over the river. The bridge uses the original masonry piers erected in 1859 during the early days of the Louisville & Nashville Railroad.

Cumberland River Greenway in downtown Nashville

The greenway soon reaches a junction. The Downtown Connector heads west away from the river to the Bicentennial Capitol Mall, the nineteen-acre state park featuring lots of green space, fountains, an amphitheater, and a variety of historical exhibits. The mall opened in Tennessee's bicentennial year, 1996. The east side of the mall is planted in vegetation indigenous to the three "Grand Divisions" of Tennessee, East, Middle, and West, each with its own plot.

The mall is presided over by Tennessee's dignified State Capitol perched high on the hill. It was completed in 1859 and is regarded as one of the nation's finest examples of Greek Revival architecture. The connector has interpretive signs explaining the history of the area. Nashville's intriguing Farmer's Market is on the opposite side of the mall, and with its food court loaded with delicious places to eat, the market makes a nice place to stop for a break.

Gone but Not Forgotten

Several animals that once made their homes in the Nashville area disappeared soon after settlement due to over-hunting and habitat destruction. Middle Tennessee is home to the Buffalo River, the Elk River, and many creeks named Panther, Wolf, and Bear. Bear still inhabit the mountains of East Tennessee, and elk and wolf have been reintroduced there, but return of these species to Davidson County is not likely. They need larger pieces of uninterrupted habitat than exist in Nashville.

People claim to see panthers every once in a while, but wildlife biologists doubt that they are really panthers. The buffalo that inhabited the area was the woodland bison. These large animals migrated to the Great Salt Lick, or French Lick, at the site of today's Bicentennial Mall just north of the State Capitol, and most of the major roads radiating out of downtown Nashville follow the routes of buffalo paths. The buffalo that were here when the early settlers arrived in 1779 were pretty much gone by 1800.

Gray wolf fed off bison and elk, and when the wolves lost their food source they turned to domestic calves, which made wolves a target for extermination. Wolves were eradicated by 1920. Panthers were killed off for the same reason.

From the junction with the mall connector, the Cumberland River Greenway threads its way 1.5 miles through several industries along the eastern edges of Germantown and Salemtown.

There is a connector from the main greenway to Morgan Park in Germantown, home to many of the German immigrants who flocked to Nashville after the U.S. Civil War. Morgan Park was established on the site of a former beer garden to provide recreation space for families of workers in this part of town that is still a mix of industrial and residential uses. The connector is named the "Magdeburg Connector" in honor of Nashville's German sister city. Interpretive signs at Morgan Park describe the sulfur spring whose waters were offered to "promote longevity, cure hangovers, and repel rats."

The paved trail continues downstream from the Magdeburg Connector to meet the greenway segment atop the MetroCenter Levee just downstream from the I-65 bridge.

CUMBERLAND RIVER GREENWAY: METROCENTER LEVEE

Brief Description: Paved trail atop Cumberland River levee, public art
Location: North Nashville: MetroCenter off Rosa Parks (US 41A) and Ed Temple Boulevards
Facilities: Paved trail, wildlife observation sites
Management: Metro Parks

Area Description

A levee runs for three miles along the inside of one of the nine sweeping Cumberland River bends from the I-65 bridge to the Martin Luther King Bridge (Clarksville Pike-US 41A), keeping dry the MetroCenter development where 12,000 people work and the Tennessee Titans NFL team practices and has its offices. Through ingenious planning and cooperation between the Corps of Engineers and Metro Parks, a three-mile paved greenway trail was added to the top of the levee during a major renovation. This level section of the greenway is adorned with some pleasing aquatic-themed public art and is a popular place for MetroCenter workers to take their breaks.

The unobstructed views of the river make this a unique place to walk, run, skate, and bike and a good place to watch the birds that are drawn to the river. Common species are American bittern, spotted sandpiper, and common snipe. Ducks that frequent the Cumberland include mallard, blue-winged teal, northern pintail, northern shoveler, gadwall, American wigeon, redhead, ring-necked, and lesser scaup.

An extension of the greenway runs one mile from the MLK Bridge to a trailhead on Ed Temple Boulevard and the campus of Tennessee State University.

CUMBERLAND RIVER GREENWAY: BROOKMEADE PARK AT KELLY'S POINT BATTLEFIELD

Brief Description: Cumberland River overlook
Location: West Nashville: near intersection of Charlotte Pike (US 70) and Davidson Road
Facilities: Paved trail, wildlife observation site
Management: Metro Parks

Area Description

This short greenway with a long name offers easy access to a remarkably unspoiled secluded overlook on the Cumberland River across from Bells Bend. The one-third-mile paved trail departs from the commercial clutter lining Charlotte Pike in a grove of trees that includes some tall cedar and expansive chinquapin oak. The trail follows a colonnade of trees, including ubiquitous hackberry and eastern red cedar, down the narrow valley of Davidson Branch to the river. The small wetland off the trail is home to the familiar cattail as well as black willow. The peaceful river overlook is flanked by some big trees, including chinquapin oak, northern red oak, sugar maple, and box elder.

This spot was not always so peaceful. During the days leading up to the Civil War Battle of Nashville in December 1864, there was an engagement here between land-based Confederate artillery and Federal gunboats in the river. Details of the battle are on an excellent interpretative sign.

This greenway was donated by JDN, the real estate developer that built the adjacent big box shopping area.

BELLS BEND PARK

Brief Description: *Cumberland River bank, forest, fields, and wetlands*
Location: *South of Scottsboro: off Old Hickory Boulevard*
Facilities: *Hiking trails, mountain bike trail, wildlife observation site, boat ramp nearby, primitive campsites, nature-outdoor center, restrooms*
Management: *Metro Parks*

Area Description

Middle Tennessee's landscape is at its finest at the intersection of ecoregions, and that is found in this 808-acre preserve in the next-to-the-last of the nine Cumberland River bends in Nashville-Davidson County. As the river straightens out and flows into Cheatham County, it slices through the uplands of the Western Highland Rim. This ecoregion intersection accounts for the tall forested ridges that form a constant backdrop at Bells Bend Park. They are pieces of the Highland Rim.

The park itself is an undulating landscape of former open cropland and pasture and rows of trees along old fencerows, ravines, and the riverbank. About a third of the park is in the Cumberland's flood plain. Several intermittent streams flow to the river, and there are wetlands within the acreage. As early as February, visitors can hear the frogs singing in one of the eight ponds. Under the leadership of Friends of Bells Bend Park, shorebird ponds along the river are being installed to replace habitat lost due to the dams on the river.

There are 7.4 miles of primitive trail at Bells Bend Park as well as a beginners' mountain bike trail.

Bells Bend Park

Bells Bend is a haven for such animal species common in Davidson County as deer, turkey, beaver, bobcat, coyote, and fox, and one not so common, the fox squirrel. It is the birds, though, that grab most of the attention at Bells Bend Park. Visitors to this quiet landscape are greeted with a cacophony of songs.

Some of the fields that were until early in the twenty-first century planted In corn and soybeans are being left to revert to their natural habitat. For many years to come, this will provide a place to observe the conversion from field-to-forest through "succession" (see p. 12). Other fields will be mowed periodically to retain an early successional habitat that is favored by several bird species such as bobwhite quail. Visitors are likely to hear their familiar "bob-white" call on a spring visit, and in the evenings during warmer months, the lovely song of the whip-poor-will. Several bird species that are uncommon in the Nashville area visit this habitat. These include dickcissel, which is rarely seen in Middle Tennessee, Henslow's sparrow, a very rare spring and fall migrant, and northern harrier.

Other birds spotted at Bells Bend are red-shouldered hawk, bald eagle, sandhill crane, and peregrine falcon, as well as the usual assortment of woodpecker and wren. The rare whooping crane makes an appearance in the bend every now and then. These big birds, the tallest in North America, were once on the brink of extinction. Even now, there are only about 500 of them, so it causes a stir when they visit Bells Bend in the winter.

Bald Eagles Return

The impounded Cumberland River is ideal habitat for bald eagles. They like large bodies of water where there are plenty of fish to eat and trees in which to nest and roost. Nevertheless, nesting bald eagles vanished from the Nashville area in the 1950s and wintering eagles became increasingly hard to find during the next decades. That all changed in the 1990s when bald eagles were reintroduced along the Cumberland River at Bells Bend.

This occurred through a process called "hacking." It involves putting eight-week-old birds in caged platforms, then releasing them at twelve weeks with the hope that they will return to the area to nest. Over a period of three years, pairs of male and female bald eagles were brought from Alaska and released along the river. Just as hoped, some of the pairs did return to Bells Bend to nest. They now come back every year and raise their chicks, usually two to a nest. Bald eagles have also been spotted at Radnor Lake and Peeler Park.

Bells Bend's more open sun-drenched land also provides a home to plants, wildflowers in particular, unlike those that grace Middle Tennessee's deep woods and unlike those found in the rocky cedar glades. Early summer flowers include butterfly weed, trumpet creeper, passionflower, yellow sundrop, and milkweed. In late summer and fall the fields glow with ironweed, goldenrod, aster, Jerusalem artichoke, and both white and yellow wingstem.

The clumps of trees are filled with northern red oak, beech, chinquapin oak, and sugar maple. Burr oak is not common in the Nashville area, but it can be found at Bells Bend, as can green ash, also not common in the area. The old fencerows are lined with hackberry, Osage orange, and silver maple, while sycamore, silver maple, cottonwood, and box elder flank the river.

The Buchanan farmhouse still stands on the parkland, the earliest portion of which dates to 1840.

The genesis of this park had its origin in something quite different: a dump. The unsuitability of the area for a landfill soon became apparent, and thanks in large part to citizens living in the area, the dump plan was dumped. Mayor Phil Bredesen arranged for the local government to purchase the land, and his successor, Mayor Bill Purcell, in 1999 had the land transferred to Metro Parks. It opened to the public in 2007.

The origin of the name "Bells Bend" is obscure. The best guess is that it takes its name from famed ironmaster Montgomery Bell (1769-1855), who before 1850 owned more than 6,000 acres here. Others believe that the name comes from landowner John Bell, who in 1840 built the original part of the Buchanan house. The bend was originally named White's Bend for pioneer settler James White. The last of the nine Cumberland River bends in Davidson County, the one opposite Bells Bend to the west, is still called White's Bend.

Birding at Bells Bend Park
Sandy Bivens

Birding at Bells Bend is a treat for me all year long! Summertime is the busy breeding season and a great time to see and hear colorful indigo buntings, orchard orioles, and yellow-breasted chats. Spring and fall migration offers an opportunity to watch an amazing diversity of species just passing through the bend on their long journey north and south.

Winter showcases the spectacular twilight "skydance" courtship display of the American woodcock flying three hundred feet in the air and dropping quickly to the ground to impress his mate. Bells Bend Park is perhaps the best place in Nashville to watch this natural phenomenon.

Bells Bend Park is much more than a place for me to work as a natural resource professional. It is a place I return to for nurture and refreshment. It offers a protected place to stand quietly at sunset and connect with the natural world.

_____

Sandy Bivens served as Superintendent of Nature Centers for Metro Parks.

INNER CENTRAL BASIN

The Inner Central Basin is the geographic heart of Tennessee. It stretches from near Lebanon on the north to Shelbyville and Lewisburg on the south with Murfreesboro at its center. The southeast quadrant of Davidson County lies within it. The Inner Basin is a mixture of flatlands and low hills underlain with Ordovician-age limestone, with outcrops of bare or nearly bare rock. Streams flow at a low gradient, often over bedrock so flat that it looks like pavement. Average elevation is 600 feet.

Before it was the target of reckless harvesting to make pencils, much of the Inner Basin was covered in stands of tall eastern red cedar. Thickets of smaller cedar still cover much of the Inner Basin, and the largest eastern red cedar forest in the world is at the combination state park and forest at Cedars of Lebanon, a few miles east of the county line in neighboring Wilson County. Where soil depth permits it, there are stands of hardwood where several types of oak and hickory are the dominant species.

The landscape of the Inner Basin is a type called *Karst* for a similar area in Italy and Slovenia. Sinks, caves, disappearing streams, dry creek beds, and underground drainage characterize it. These features are created when slightly acidic groundwater dissolves the limestone bedrock. This phenomenon of underground passages can be observed at Long Hunter State Park's Couchville Lake. When J. Percy Priest Lake was impounded, water moving through underground passages filled a depression away from the reservoir, creating the smaller lake. The water level of 110-acre Couchville Lake always matches the level of the bigger lake, which is the source of Couchville Lake's water.

Caves and their openings are havens for wildlife. Raccoons and rodents move in and out of them, and some birds, such as the eastern phoebe, make their nests in the openings. The dark caves are home to gray bats, salamanders, cavefish, and blind cave crayfish. The rare Tennessee cave salamander is found only in a handful of caves.

The cedar glades of the *Karst* landscape are the most interesting natural features of the Inner Central Basin. Called "cedar" because they are in cedar forests, glades are rocky arid openings where the soil is too shallow for trees to take root (see p. 14).

The most unnatural feature of the Inner Central Basin is J. Percy Priest Lake. It was created in the 1960s when the Corps of Engineers (COE) dammed up the Stones River seven miles upstream from where it empties into the Cumberland. This destroyed the most scenic part of the Stones River and flooded—in the name of flood control—thousands of acres of the unique Inner Basin ecosystem. But at the same time it created a watery wildlife habitat. The COE acquired a 10,000-acre buffer around the 213-mile shoreline to keep much of the cedar-covered landscape in its natural state.

The COE, State Parks, and Metro Parks manage the nature parks around the lake. J. Percy Priest, for whom the dam and lake are named, was a local member of Congress who advocated for construction of the dam in the late 1940s.

LONG HUNTER STATE PARK

Brief Description: *Lakeshore, cedar and hardwood forests, fields, and cedar glades*
Location: *J. Percy Priest Lake, east shore: off Hobson Pike (TN 171) south of I-40 Mt. Juliet exit*

Facilities: *Paved trail, hiking trails, mountain bike trails, wildlife observation sites, boat ramp, visitor center, restrooms*
Management: *State Parks*

Area Description

This 2,400-acre park extending along thirty miles of J. Percy Priest Lake shore protects samples of the distinctive natural features of Middle Tennessee's Inner Central Basin. Level trails wander through oak-hickory forests, cedar woods, bluffs above the submerged course of the Stones River, and some outstanding cedar glades that are unique to the region.

A cedar glade at Long Hunter State Park

The state park has a plentiful deer population, so visitors are almost guaranteed to see one. Raccoon and possum are common at Long Hunter as well. Bobcats and foxes are harder to find, but they are there, making their homes in the openings in the *Karst* limestone landscape and along the bluffs of the submerged river bed. However, they are elusive, and it is a rare visitor who spots one.

Some of the twenty species of waterfowl that winter at Long Hunter can be observed by walking along Couchville Lake and J. Percy Priest's sheltered coves. There are also resident shorebirds like the great blue heron, Tennessee's largest nesting bird. Gulls populate the lakes too, with the most common being the ring-billed gull. Others spotted at Long Hunter are Bonaparte's gull, laughing gull, herring gull, and the extremely rare great black-backed gull.

There are about 135 species of butterflies in Tennessee, and seventy-six have been spotted at Long Hunter. The park provides a checklist, as well as one for the sixty-nine species of dragonflies and damselflies.

The most popular walk is around Couchville Lake on the paved two-mile trail. It is home to the Couchville Lake Arboretum, a project of Friends of Long Hunter State Park that identifies forty-four trees. A brochure is available at the visitor center and on the park's website.

The visitor center, Couchville Lake, Nature Loop Trail, Inland Trail and Deer Trail are east of Hobson Pike (TN 171). The four-mile Bryant Grove Trail extends from Couchville Lake to the Bryant Grove Recreation Area up the lake, passing through hardwoods, cedar woods, and an expansive cedar glade. From the Baker Grove parking area west of the highway, the Volunteer Trail parallels the shore six miles to a primitive campsite where camping is allowed with a permit that can be obtained at the visitor center. A popular hike is to combine a portion of the Volunteer Trail with the Day Loop that runs off it. The walk of 4.1 miles offers bluff-top views of the lake, interesting rock formations, and a rich oak-hickory forest. The Volunteer Trail gets its name from the Boy Scouts and other volunteers who constructed it.

Mountain biking is available on the Jones Mill Trail at Bryant Grove. The trail is in two loops, one of two miles and the other of four miles.

The name for this park comes from the hunters who ventured into the Cumberland country from colonial America in the 1760-70s. They would stay for long periods, hence their name. Uriah Stone was on the earliest recorded expedition in 1767. He struggled in a canoe forty miles up the tributary of the Cumberland River that has been known as Stones River ever since.

COUCHVILLE CEDAR GLADE STATE NATURAL AREA

Brief Description: *Forest and cedar glade*
Location: *Adjacent to Long Hunter State Park: off Mt. Juliet Road*
Facilities: *Hiking trail*
Management: *State Parks*

Area Description

This 122-acre natural area adjoining Long Hunter State Park protects the world's largest known population of the Tennessee coneflower, a magnificently beautiful plant that was until 2011 a federally-listed endangered species. The Couchville Glade was one of only five known populations of the flower when the natural area was established, and a meander through the area in June when the flowers are in bloom is sight to behold. Other rare plants in the glade include the Tennessee milk-vetch, shaggy dwarf morning glory, Gattinger's lobelia, limestone fameflower, pale umbrellawort, and savory. In addition to the ubiquitous cedar, there is a mature oak-hickory forest made up of shagbark hickory and chinquapin, shumard, white, and post oak. The bright yellow butterflies seen darting around are the southern dogface, so named because of their wing pattern resembling the face of a dog.

Comeback Kids

Visitors are almost guaranteed to spot a deer in Nashville's preserves, particularly early in the morning or late in the afternoon. The Tennessee deer population is just under one million, and though it is hard to believe, this most popular game animal was once on the verge of extinction in the Volunteer State. It was estimated in 1940 that there were only 250 in the whole state, and they were limited to the remote mountains of East Tennessee. White-tailed deer now inhabit all of Tennessee's ninety-five counties as a result of the restoration effort of the Tennessee Wildlife Resources Agency (TWRA).

Another animal likely to be spotted in the Davidson County outdoors is the wild turkey. It too was near extinction in Tennessee before a TWRA restoration program was started in 1954, and today the wild turkey population in the state is in excess of 75,000.

The majestic bald eagle was absent from the Nashville area for many years, a victim of the pesticide DDT, but our national bird has been successfully reintroduced and can be spotted along the Cumberland River and occasionally at Radnor Lake (see p. 44).

The osprey is another large fish-eating raptor that just about vanished from Tennessee due to DDT, and it too has made a comeback. Nesting ospreys have been spotted on Old Hickory Lake, and ospreys have been seen on Mill Creek.

River otters were once common throughout the United States, but by the 1940s, their range in Tennessee was limited to a few places in West Tennessee. Thanks to a successful TWRA restoration program started in the 1980s, the elusive playful creatures are back, and can be seen in the Harpeth River watershed.

The Tennessee coneflower, unique to Middle Tennessee's Inner Central Basin, was listed as an endangered species in 1979, but recovered to such an extent that it was removed from the list in 2011.

All of this can be enjoyed on a level trail that winds slightly less than a mile and is named in memory of Tyler Sykes who worked for this area's preservation.

Friends of Long Hunter State Park on the annual "mega hike"

When this rare habitat was threatened by the rampant development in this part of Davidson and adjoining Wilson Counties, The Nature Conservancy in 1994 stepped in and purchased the first forty-three acres with financial help from American Airlines, Cracker Barrel, and the former Bell South. The area is managed by the staff of Long Hunter State Park.

Sensing the Couchville Cedar Glade
Rita Venable

It was not love at first sight. I crunched out of my car onto a gravel parking lot at Couchville Glade and squinted down the grassy trail to the wooded respite ahead. On a field trip with a native plant group, I wondered how well I knew these folks.

The shaded woods were not the Holy Grail today, so we moved on to what looked like another gravel parking lot. There were cedar trees standing all around like sentinels. My fellow trekkers turned into Zen-people searching the ground. How could this many people lose their car keys at one time?

Then I began to see what they saw, and, in time, I came back again and again and fell in love with the glades. By March the long-styled glade cress with its almond-scented perfume already seduces butterflies without blushing. Eastern Commas make fools of themselves, falling over backwards, lying on the ground and still trying to nectar on plants too small to support them. In April the Nashville Breadroot sports its violet suit. May presents the pink rays of the Tennessee coneflower, the first federally endangered plant species listed in Tennessee.

It was the scents, though, that elevated the glades and me beyond admiration. I was on my knees photographing a great spangled fritillary when I first breathed the minty sweet fragrance of glade savory. Whenever the sun warms the cedars and I crush the needles, I close my eyes and time-travel back to my childhood in Nashville and the cedar trees my family decorated at Christmas.

The eastern red cedar is my favorite tree. It grows stubbornly on rock cliffs, along interstates, in swamps—just about everywhere in Tennessee. It comes up wild in most people's yards, because songbirds eat the berries and make free tree deposits. The bright green juniper hairstreak caterpillar eats the needles, forms a chrysalis and turns into a thumb-nail sized green dazzler.

Sometimes I stand in the quiet of the glades and think about these ancient rock beds formed from the shallow seas that covered this area 500 million years ago when only God walked the earth and sea creatures like cephalopods, bryozoans, and brachiopods swam in the warm waters. When they died they sunk to the bottom and froze in time as fossils.

It's these rocks that cause the temperature of the open glades to range 10-30 degrees hotter than the surrounding woods. It's not surprising that spring comes earlier here, summer seems hotter, and fall lingers longer. The plants and animals that make up the cedar glades thrive in what we perceive as hardship. In places the soil is less than two inches deep. Put some of these plants in deep, rich soils that we think would improve their lot, and they would die. They flourish where they are meant to be.

Now, instead of comparing cedar glades to parking lots, I can hardly step onto hot gravel anywhere without wondering about what's going on at the cedar glades. I even get a little Zen-like myself when I go to the glades. It comes with the territory.

_____

Rita Venable is a nature writer and photographer active in the North American Butterfly Association.

COOK RECREATION AREA

Brief Description: *Forest and cedar glade*
Location: *J. Percy Priest Lake, east shore: south of I-40 Old Hickory Boulevard (TN 45) exit*
Facilities: *Hiking trail, boat ramp, restrooms*
Management: *Corps of Engineers*

Area Description

This area on the eastern shore of J. Percy Priest Lake offers a microcosm of the Inner Basin landscape. The natural features are best enjoyed along the 1½-mile figure-eight Three Hickories Trail. Along it are stands of hardwood dominated by variety oak and hickory, clumps of cedar, open cedar glades, limestone rock outcrops, sinkholes, and carpets of soft mosses. There are also remnants of human habitation, including a stone fence. Among the flowers that bloom in the glades are pale blue glade phlox, psoralea, and Gattinger's petalostemon. Birds love the successional habitat, and among those to be enjoyed are the red-bellied woodpecker, great-crested flycatcher, and towhee, as well as the shorebirds and waterfowl on the lake.

The trail starts near the picnic area. If that area is closed, the trail can be accessed directly across the main road from the entrance to the old campground. The trail goes off to the right approaching the boat ramp. Getting to the area takes some doing, as the route follows remnants of several roads blocked by the lake.

Neotropical Migrant Birds

Many of the bird species inhabiting Nashville's natural areas are labeled "Neotropical migrants" because they spend part of the year in the tropics. They nest in North America but spend the winter months in Mexico, the Caribbean, and Central and South America. Neotropical migrants make up about 350 of the 600 bird species in the United States and Canada. There are around seventy species of the migrants in Tennessee, and they start arriving around March or April, with purple martins, swallows, and swifts the first to arrive. Among the forest-loving migrants who inhabit our woods are thrushes, warblers, flycatchers, and tanagers. The deep blue indigo bunting is one of the most commonly sighted Neotropical migrants. The tiny hummingbird is another.

The habitat requirements for Neotropical migrants vary by species. Some like deep hardwood forests, some like pine plantations, and some like old fields. The loss of open land to development is reducing habitat and leading to a corresponding decline in the number of Neotropical migrants spotted each year.

MOUNT VIEW GLADE STATE NATURAL AREA

Brief Description: Cedar glade
Location: Mount View Road off Murfreesboro Road (US 41-70S)
Facilities: Hiking trail
Management: State Parks

Area Description

This area of about twenty acres may be small, but it packs plenty of scenery, particularly in the large open glade that is home to a colony of Tennessee coneflower. In addition to the big glade, which is dotted with perfectly shaped green cedar, there are several smaller glades and a forest of cedar and small hardwoods. Other rare species found at the natural area are glade-cress, Tennessee milk-vetch, glade phlox, limestone fame-flower, and glade-onion.

The Nature Conservancy purchased this land in 1990 and donated it to the State. An unmarked trail wanders through the property from the tiny parking lot on Mount View Road.

ANDERSON ROAD RECREATION AREA

Brief Description: Lakeshore, forest, and cedar glade
Location: J. Percy Priest Lake, west shore: off Bell Road
Facilities: Paved trail, hiking trail, wildlife observation sites, boat
    ramp, restrooms
Management: Corps of Engineers

Area Description

This COE-managed area covers the tip of a peninsula in J. Percy Priest Lake created by the embayments of Hamilton and

Smith Springs Creeks. The area consists of a cedar forest with some hardwoods mixed in and a magnificent cedar glade in the middle. In places the hardwoods are even-aged stands of shagbark hickory, recognized by the hanging bark.

The loop trail around the peninsula is called the "Anderson Road Fitness Trail," a wide paved trail indistinguishable from a Metro Parks greenway trail. Rocky side paths lead through the deep green canopy to the lakeshore where there are benches for enjoying views of the lake's broad expanse. Twenty species of waterfowl winter on the lake. Tennessee's largest bird, the great blue heron, is a common sight.

The paved trail of slightly more than a mile does not quite make a circle, so the last bit of the return is on the dead-end stub of Anderson Road. A rocky level path loops away from the dead-end of Anderson Road near the fitness trail parking lot and meets the paved trail at the far end where it comes out on Anderson Road. The primitive trail bisects a sprawling cedar glade and meanders through the rocky landscape that is dotted with clumps of cedar surrounded by carpets of brilliant green moss. The open glade is a riot of color in the spring, particularly in April. There is an abundance of yellow primrose, Nashville breadroot, glade sandwort, yellow stargrass, phlox, and prickly pear cactus, which usually blooms in May and June.

HAMILTON CREEK PARK

Brief Description: *Lakeshore, cedar and hardwood forests, and cedar glade*
Location: *J. Percy Priest Lake, west shore: off Bell Road*
Facilities: *Mountain bike trails, boat ramp, restrooms*
Management: *Metro Parks*

Area Description

Hamilton Creek Park takes up 790 acres of classic Inner Basin terrain on the west shore of J. Percy Priest Lake opposite the east shore's Long Hunter State Park. In addition to its marina for sailboats, Hamilton Creek Park is best known for nearly ten miles of mountain bike trails. But its natural features should not be overlooked. The lower elevations are covered in places by uncommonly tall cedars standing straight as matchsticks. The higher elevations are covered with a typical oak-hickory forest.

The park's backwoods is in two parts, one north and one south of Bell Road. The trailhead for the 6-mile Pinnacle Trail is north of Bell Road off Ned Shelton Road, and the trailhead for the 2.5-mile Lakeside Trail is south of Bell Road off the main park entrance. A subway under Bell Road connects the two wandering trails. The trails can be used for walking as well as mountain biking, but walkers should yield to the cyclists. Metro Parks has done a good job of getting mountain bikers to stop using hiking trails in other parks, so the mountain bikers have priority at Hamilton Creek.

Hamilton Creek Park is home to a rare plant species, the leafy prairie-clover. Its range is limited to a few sites in the Inner Central Basin and in Alabama and Illinois. The leafy prairie clover's clusters of small purple flowers show themselves in August. It grows in the grassy glades off the road leading to the Lakeside trailhead. These mini-meadows hold more soil than the rocky glades and as a result, retain more water. After a big rain, the soil is damp and spongy. A wet weather stream flows through one of them. These areas are quite fragile, so they should be enjoyed from the road.

Endangered Species

The U.S. Fish and Wildlife Service currently lists these
   endangered species in Davidson County:
Nashville crayfish—*Orconectes shoupi*
Dromedary pearlymussel—*Dromus dromas*
Tuberculed-blossom pearlymussel—*Epioblasma torulosa*
Tan riffleshell—*Epioblasma florentina walkeri*
Orangefoot pimpleback—*Plethobasus cooperianus*
White wartyback pearlymussel—*Plethobasus cicatricous*
Pough pigtow—*Pleurobema plenum*
Price's potato-bean—*Apios priceana*
Short's bladderpod—*Lesquerella glabosa*
Cumberlandian combshell—*Epioblasma brevidens*
Pyne's ground-plum—*Astragalus bibullatus*
Braun's rock-cress—*Arabis perstellata*

Hamilton Creek Park rests on land acquired by the COE for
J. Percy Priest Lake and leased to Metro Parks.

MILL CREEK GREENWAY

Brief Description: Sections of linear park along a major Cumberland
   River tributary
Location: Antioch and Cane Ridge: Ezell Park off Harding Place
   (TN 255), Blue Hole Road, Old Hickory Boulevard, and off
   Nolensville Road (US 31A-41A)
Facilities: Paved trail, canoe access
Management: Metro Parks

Area Description

Mill Creek meanders from its source near Nolensville across southeast Davidson County before giving its waters to the Cumberland River opposite Shelby Bottoms. Though the long creek runs through some intensely developed areas, except for a few places where it has been channelized, the creek corridor has held up well and is a haven for a variety of wildlife that can be observed from the greenway or by floating the stream when the water level is right for it.

Long-range plans call for a greenway along Mill Creek's entire length in Davidson County, and three segments are open as of this writing. A 1.5-mile segment runs from near Lenox Village off Nolensville Road (US 31A-41A) to Old Hickory Boulevard in the Cane Ridge neighborhood; a 1.8-mile-segment starts off Blue Hole Road near Antioch Middle School; and a 1.25-mile segment starts at Ezell Park upstream from the creek's crossing of Harding Place (TN 255), west of the International Airport.

Metro Parks has acquired land between the first two segments downstream from Old Hickory Boulevard and will build a segment to connect with the first segment. And there will soon be a section downstream from Thompson Lane.

Mill Creek is a floatable steam when it not too high to be dangerous or too low to be impassable. There is access at Old Hickory Boulevard, Ezell Park, and Thompson Lane. Mill Creek is included on the list of streams being designated as blueways by the Tennessee Scenic Rivers Association, and the waterway gets a little tender love and care each spring when the association conducts its annual cleanup.

2010 Floods

On Saturday and Sunday, May 1 and 2, 2010, the Nashville area received the most rainfall ever recorded in a single stretch, officially 13.57 inches at the International Airport and officially 18.04 inches in parts of the Harpeth River watershed, though some private measurements reached 21 inches. To put that in perspective, the maximum rainfall recorded on the Gulf Coast during Hurricane Katrina in 2005 was 16.43 inches. The Nashville area rainfall was equivalent to 420 *billion* gallons of water.

The Harpeth River at Bellevue crested at 33 feet, 13 feet above flood stage, shattering the previous record of 24.3 feet set on February 13, 1948. The Cumberland River in downtown Nashville crested at 51.86 feet, nearly 12 feet above flood stage, breaking the old record of 47.6 feet.

The flood was a disaster of epic proportion, claiming twenty-one lives, including ten in Davidson County, and causing in excess of $2 billion in property damage in Nashville alone. With every tragedy, though, comes opportunity, and the May 2010 floods were no exception. There was an overwhelming outpouring of help in both rescue and reconstruction. And there was no looting.

Nashville's greenways and nature parks did not escape damage, and the same volunteerism that characterized the community at large was present in the parks and preserves. At Radnor Lake, for example, some 3,600 volunteers performed recovery work, including rebuilding trails that were ruined by some of the forty landslides in the state natural area. Another opportunity was presented by removal of houses from flood-prone areas, houses that never should have been allowed there in the first place. Areas along Mill, Richland, and Whites Creeks will now be left as green space connected to greenways.

In East Nashville, the flood damage to the small airport adjacent to Shelby Bottoms named for famed pilot Cornelia Fort made it feasible for 135 acres to be added to the greenway and nature park.

Mill Creek is a real "diamond in the rough." Those who explore it, as opposed to merely rushing past it on Interstates 24 and 40, will be amazed by its natural features. A short stretch upstream from I-40 is practically devoid of development and represents a significant natural area surrounded by urbanization. There is a fifteen-acre island that is home to one of only two Middle Tennessee rookeries for the black-crowned night heron. Thanks to the efforts of the Tennessee Wildlife Resources Agency and private landowners working with The Land Trust for Tennessee, this patch of Nashville will remain forever green.

Common trees along the greenway are sycamore, cherry, cedar, and wild pear. In the less developed areas along the creek, there are white oak and red oak estimated to be in excess of 250 years old. The creek side is home to a variety of wildflowers, including phlox, bloodroot, spring beauty, Jack-in-the-pulpit, Dutchmen's britches, and several kinds of trillium.

The hourglass patterns cut into trees on the stream bank are evidence of beavers living along the creek. The otters that inhabit the lower reaches of the creek are more elusive. Visitors are likely to spot kingfishers, mockingbirds, cardinals, and wrens, as well as bluebirds that take to the boxes built for them. Several species of ducks like Mill Creek's waters, as do great blue heron, Tennessee largest nesting bird. Bald eagles and ospreys are sometimes spotted trying to make a meal out of fish. Owls are mostly nocturnal, but they are there, and there is almost always a red-tailed hawk soaring above or perched on a limb. There are also coopers hawks, kestrels, and woodcocks. Red foxes den in the crevices along the bluffs.

Those willing to take a closer look at Mill Creek will find a species of aquatic life that doesn't exist anywhere else in the world: *Orconectes shoupi*, popularly known as the Nashville Crayfish. Because it is only found in the Mill Creek watershed, and because the watershed has been so substantially degraded, the Nashville Crayfish is on the federal endangered species list.

CANE RIDGE PARK

Brief Description: *Forest, fields, and wetland*
Location: *Cane Ridge: off Burkett Road between Nolensville Road (US 31A-41A) and I-24*
Facilities: *Paved trail, hiking trail, mountain bike trail, restroom*
Management: *Metro Parks*

Area Description

This 280-acre park is a mosaic of developed recreation sites, open fields, and forest. Its location on the very boundary where the flatter cedar-studded-Inner Central Basin meets the rolling Outer Basin as well as the one-hundred-foot elevation difference and part of the park's past life as a dairy farm pasture, all guarantee a wide variety of habitat. A paved walking trail circles the softball fields, and the roads offer a serene place to walk when they are not too busy.

The park's upper area holds a mature forest of sugar maple, red and white oak, ash, cherry, and tulip poplar while the lower part is home to a forest dominated by hackberry, elm, and the ubiquitous cedar so common in the Inner Basin. There are a few rocky glades. The beautiful little cattail-filled wetland on the park's northern edge produces a chorus of singing frogs. Wildflowers in the upper area include bloodroot, trout lily, toothwort, violets, May apple, and touch-me-nots. The lower areas are home to the glade species, including stone crop, levenworthia, saxifrage, glade privet, and prickly pear cactus.

There is a rocky, hard-to-find unmarked trail leading into the woods near the parking area beyond the softball fields. It takes off by a clump of trees, descends the hill, eventually crosses a gas pipeline, and enters a residential area of LaVergne. Along the way there is a side trail that loops through the woods beneath a canopy of surprisingly large elm, sugar maple, and oak. This loop is faintly marked with stacks of rocks. On a spring walk, visitors can enjoy several blooming flowers, including spring beauty, purple phacelia, false garlic, and prickly pear cactus. The trail passes a deep sinkhole, which is typical of the *Karst* landscape of the Inner Basin cedar country.

Cane Ridge Park is also home to a mountain bike trail. Long range plans call for extension of the bike trail into the area traversed by the primitive trail, so the trail pattern will be substantially altered.

OUTER CENTRAL BASIN

The Outer Central Basin produces the pleasing undulating mosaic of field and forest that blesses Middle Tennessee with some of the nation's loveliest pastoral countryside. Average elevation is 750 feet, but in places it rises over 1,000 feet. The highest point in Nashville is in the Outer Basin, 1,160 feet at the Radnor Lake State Natural Area.

The dominant feature of the Outer Basin in Nashville is the range of mountain-like ridges jutting across the southwestern edge of Davidson County. They are detached pieces of the Western Highland Rim, called by geologists "outliers" or "remnants," parts of the rim escarpment separated by erosion.

The forested ridges have been given the name "Harpeth Hills," for they separate the watersheds of the Cumberland River and one of its major tributaries, the Harpeth River. The eastern tip of the range is sometimes called the "Overton Hills" because the land was once owned by John Overton, whose home from the 1700s, Travellers Rest, still stands off Franklin Road (US 31) and is open to the public. The Harpeth Hills provide the setting for Nashville's most popular nature parks, Radnor Lake State Natural Area and the Warner Parks.

Because the Outer Central Basin is in a transition zone between one type of forest region on the east (mixed-mesophytic, where no one or two species dominate) and another type on the west (oak-hickory, where those two species dominate), the Outer Basin's preserves are home to an extraordinarily diverse forest. The moist north-facing slopes and deep coves harbor a forest reminiscent of what is found in the mountains of East Tennessee. Tulip poplar, beech, northern red oak, shagbark hickory, sugar maple, black cherry, dogwood, and persimmon are common. The largest sassafras tree in Tennessee is found in Percy Warner Park. The drier ridges' slopes are more reminiscent of the Western Highland Rim where common tree species include a variety of oak and hickory as well as an abundance of sourwood and blackgum. The driest south facing slopes resemble the Inner Central Basin's forest with no shortage of hackberry and cedar. The shallow-soiled ridge crests are home to chestnut oak, black oak, pignut hickory, and mountain laurel.

Most of the dense forest of the Outer Central Basin's two big parks is not old growth in the strictest sense, but it has been many decades since a saw felled a tree. There are places with trees 150 years old, and much of the forest in the Harpeth Hills' parks is "climax" (see p. 10). There is one stand of sure-enough old growth, 200-plus acres of big trees in the former Hill Tract that was added to the Warner Parks early in the twenty-first century.

Nothing delights visitors to the woods of the Harpeth Hills like the nearly year-round display of wildflowers. The hills are home to more than 400 species of blooming plants, and something can be found blooming from mid-February to mid-November.

Common Spring Wildflowers Of the Harpeth Hills

Dwarf larkspur	Cut-leaf toothwort
Rue anemone	Virginia bluebell
May apple	Daisy fleabane
Bloodroot	Jack-in-the-pulpit
Dutchman's breeches	Trout lily
Spring beauty	Toadshade trillium
Yellow violet	Sessile trillium
Common blue violet	

The Outer Basin's woods are significant breeding grounds for Neotropical migrant birds, which make up about forty of the 113 breeding birds of the Central Basin (see p. 56). In all, close to 200 bird species have been spotted in the Harpeth Hills. The forest also hosts seventy-one amphibians and reptiles and forty-six mammals. Of the 135 butterfly species in Tennessee, eighty-seven are found in Davidson County, a further testament to the area's ecological diversity.

Wet weather springs are an interesting feature of the Harpeth Hills. During and after rains, water seeps through soil and porous rock until it reaches a shelf of impermeable bedrock. The water then migrates laterally, emerging from the surface as a spring. After a big rain visitors are treated to impromptu mini-waterfalls where the discharge from the springs tumbles over rocks.

Outside the steep forested Harpeth Hills, the Outer Basin in Nashville is a rolling terrain of mostly developed land, but with some surprisingly undeveloped areas, particularly in a few of the broad Cumberland River bends and one bend in the Stones River. (Greenways and parks in the Cumberland bends are described in the Cumberland River chapter.). The tree-lined smaller waterways are given to flooding, so development has for the most part stayed away from their banks. It is along those streams where some of Nashville's nicest greenways are found.

STONES RIVER GREENWAY

Brief Description: Linear Park along Stones and Cumberland Rivers and across two river bends

Location: Donelson and Hermitage: both sides of Lebanon Road (US 70) and McGavock Pike, Heartland Park, and Briley Parkway (TN 155) at Two Rivers Park

Facilities: Paved trail, connections to trailheads, canoe access, restrooms at Two Rivers Park
Management: Metro Parks

Area Description

This long and varied greenway extends nine miles from J. Percy Priest Dam on the Stones River to Two Rivers Park overlooking the Cumberland River near the Opryland complex. The riverside section along the Stones River offers one of the nicest walks and bike rides in Nashville and has become a favorite of residents of the Donelson-Hermitage area. The spectacular pedestrian bridge across the Cumberland River (see p. 28) links the Stones River Greenway at Two Rivers Park to the Shelby Bottoms Greenway in East Nashville, creating a continuous twelve-mile paved greenway route.

Music City Bikeway

Nashville is on a mission to make itself more bicycle friendly, a task that is not easy because of the automobile-dependant way Nashville has grown. Part of the mission has been accomplished by the development of the Music City Bikeway that travels 26.07 miles from the Deep Well entrance to Percy Warner Park on Highway 100 to the J. Percy Priest Dam on the Stones River, dubbed the "Percy-to-Percy Ride." The bikeway follows greenways for 14.1 miles, dedicated bike lanes on streets for 7 miles, and roadway shared with motor vehicles for 5 miles. The route can be identified by the distinctive green-and-white sign featuring a bicycle above piano keys. Maps and other information are available at *www.nashville.gov/bikeways*.

The Stones River Greenway is in three distinct parts: along the Stones River downstream from the dam, across a horseshoe bend near the river's mouth, and across the Cumberland River's Pennington Bend. Spurs lead to the main greenway from Stewarts Ferry Pike near the Tennessee School for the Blind and from Lebanon Road (US 70) at the YMCA. The greenway trail gets across busy Lebanon Road by passing under the road's river bridges and then looping up to cross the river on the charming 1937 steel truss bridge.

Trees growing along the river are the same species that grow along the Cumberland. Box elder and cottonwood are common, and there a few exceptionally large sycamore and pin oak. The greenway is a haven for all manner of birds, including the water-loving birds that take to the two rivers.

The Stones River Greenway between the dam and Lebanon Road is a great place to enjoy flowering plants in the summer, including chicory, Queen Anne's lace, trumpet creeper, jewelweed, passionflower, wild potato vine, daylily, Virginia dayflower, and black-eyed Susan. There is no shortage of dragonflies in the summer as well.

Among the interesting features on this stretch of greenway are the bridge abutments from an abandoned railroad. They carried the tracks of the ambitiously named Tennessee & Pacific that connected Lebanon to Nashville. In 1902, entrepreneur Jere Baxter built a competing parallel line, the Tennessee Central, and its bridge is still in use.

Stones River Greenway upstream from Lebanon Road

The "anywhere USA" chain stores that sprawl over the broad river bottom at Lebanon Road belie the historic nature of this area. "Clover Bottom" it is called, and it is strongly associated with Andrew Jackson, whose home, The Hermitage, is a few miles to the east. Jackson had several ventures at Clover Bottom, including a racetrack, a store, and farther downstream, a boat yard. It is believed the first horse race was run here in 1799. Before Jackson arrived on the Cumberland frontier, pioneer leader John Donelson, whose daughter Rachel would marry Jackson, occupied the Clover Bottom, planting the first corn crop shortly after his party completed its perilous 1,000-mile river voyage in 1780. Even before that, long hunter

Uriah Stone in 1767 made his way up the river past the Clover Bottom on a voyage that gave the river its name.

The next section of the greenway runs along the opposite bank of the Stones River on an old road and then cuts across the big bend the river makes before emptying into the Cumberland. An imposing feature is Stone Hall, the stately 1918 Colonial Revival mansion overlooking the Stones River just downstream from Lebanon Road. The house and surrounding twelve acres had been in the Merritt family for generations, and when owner Stroud Merritt decided to sell Stone Hall, he offered it to Metro Parks. A grassroots fundraising effort that included a grant from the Memorial Foundation helped secure funds needed to accept his generous offer. Along with a charming riverside log cabin named Eversong, Stone Hall and its grounds were incorporated into the greenway with long-range plans calling for it to be a visitor center. It is on the National Register of Historic Places.

Stone Hall, built in 1918

The Pennington Bend section of the greenway runs between Heartland Park on the Stones River and Two Rivers Park overlooking the Cumberland River. Two names common in this bend are McGavock and Two Rivers; the trail runs between McGavock High and Two Rivers Middle Schools, under McGavock Pike and through Two Rivers Park. The McGavocks were prominent landowners in the1800s and gave the name Two Rivers to their splendid 1870 Italianate-style mansion that stands near the greenway and is owned by Metro Parks.

Tradition has it that Graves Pennington settled the bend after arriving with the John Donelson party in 1780.

The Stones River has been designated as a blueway (see p. 104). There are access points at J. Percy Priest Dam, Lebanon Road (US 70), and Heartland Park.

Stones River: Uniquely at the Right Place at the Right Time
Shain Dennison

Spine-tingling moments have happened for me on the Stones River Greenway more than once. Moments that feel strongly intuitive, like I'm being allowed a glimpse into the web of life, one that's of interconnected relationships and purpose, richly layered and spanning time.

Growing up in Mt. Juliet and driving Lebanon Road since I was sixteen, I traversed the old green truss bridge over the Stones River hundreds of times. Going over the bridge was itself a treat. Always, I'd stare at the mysterious old stone abutments just downstream and the narrow log cabin you can see from the bridge.

I'd wonder about the cabin, a small jewel box called Eversong that clings to the river bluff—three narrow stories tall—seeming to rise out of it. Who built it? How old is it? Was it there when the big house across the street, the old Donelson place called Stone Hall, was built?

The storybook Stone Hall sits perfectly on a hill, tucked behind dense evergreens lining Lebanon Road, giving it a sense of mystery and seclusion. Although I didn't get the nerve to drive up its curving entranceway to get close enough to see it well, I could see that it was a special place, and I had a special feeling about it.

It is the embodiment of what was to become my favorite: Colonial Revival architecture, with a porte cochere, flanking bay windows, tiled roof, and classical, romantic English embellishments, graced by lovely gardens and a wonderful old barn.

I'd think whoever built Eversong or Stone Hall had to have an eye for the siting of things and creating something special. Were they descended from the Donelsons who settled Nashville? Having had an affinity for Rachel Jackson through summer stints in high school as a tour guide at The Hermitage, Home of Andrew Jackson, I hoped there was a link.

I had an intense feeling about these places . . . more than a passing curiosity.

Fast forward . . . out of interests spawned during my teen summers at The Hermitage, I got a degree in historic preservation and work at the Metro Historical Commission soon after. As a volunteer, representing things historic, I was offered the first staff position for the Greenways Commission. This led to getting to know local artist, community leader, and former Metro Council member Phil Ponder, who led the way to receiving federal funding with the assistance of former Congressman Bob Clement to build the Stones River Greenway.

As you might guess . . . . this led to preserving the sites of my early and continued interest: the truss bridge, the old stone abutments, the cabin, and the big house!

I discovered many uncanny connections to these places during the saga of developing the Stones River Greenway and protecting Stone Hall.

There are two potential connections I'll never have time to explore, and part of me would rather keep the mystery:

One, Uriah Stone, for which the Stones River is named, traveled with a group of long hunters for which many of Middle Tennessee's rivers are named, which included Obediah Terrell, for the Obey and Obed rivers. My maiden name is Terrell. Might my *roots and love of rivers be somehow connected to him? The other, a Terrell, is reputed to have been among the Donelson party that came up the Cumberland to settle Nashville. Might I and those associated with the old Donelson place have had ancestors on the same trip?*

These connections, real or imagined, are part of the reason the Stones River Greenway is especially a favorite of mine.

There are other reasons for this greenway to hold a special place for me and others. It truly links a huge melting pot of people to each other and the scenic and natural resources of their community.

It brings joy to me and joy I see on faces of the many individuals and families on it—joy in being outdoors, along a river, and experiencing land.

It brought people together into special relationships: the late Amelia Edwards and Bob Brown, both of whom were historians, helped research and interpret the rich history of the greenway's eleven historic points of interest; and Stroud Merritt, the owner of Stone Hall (a Donelson, two ways!) who passed up an opportunity to realize more profit by agreeing at the eleventh hour to sell to Metro Parks, rather than to developers, so that Stone Hall and Eversong could be forever protected for public use and benefit.

These things are enough to make me count my blessings to enjoy worthwhile work. Being at the right time and place, able to marry two passions, historic preservation and land conservation, to help protect Stone Hall, Eversong, the old bridge, and old abutments on a greenway make me think I am doing what I am meant to do. Perhaps those early, vague feelings about these places were some kind of intuition. I'd like to think so.

Shain Dennison is Metro Parks Assistant Director for Greenways and Open Space.

Stone Hall
Nora Johnson Cantrell

Welcome to the wayside park,
All honeysuckle bound,
With table and a resting seat.

The park is thine and mine, friend,
May we enjoy and keep
It cleanly, and leave thank crumbs
For the singing birds to eat.

Welcome to the wayside park,
And should you have a Care
Within your heart, we hope you may
Forget, and leave it there.

Nora Johnson Cantrell and her husband, Dempsey Weaver Cantrell, in 1918 built Stone Hall. This poem appeared in a 1947-48 booklet of the Lebanon Road Garden Club.

SEVEN MILE CREEK GREENWAY

Brief Description: *Linear park along a restored stream*
Location: *Tusculum: off Edmonson Pike*
Facilities: *Paved trail, restrooms at Whitfield Park*
Management: *Metro Parks*

Area Description

This greenway follows the sycamore-lined banks Seven Mile Creek for one-half mile upstream from Whitfield Park along the edge of the State of Tennessee's Ellington

Agricultural Center. The greenway provides a pleasant outdoor experience for residents of the densely-populated Tusculum neighborhood on the east side of Ellington and the Crieve Hall neighborhood on the west side. (For the trail network at Ellington, see below.)

Seven Mile Creek is a major tributary of Mill Creek, and like its parent, has seen its share of degradation from random development. But like Mill Creek, it has some near-pristine sections, including this stretch where the State of Tennessee has undertaken a restoration. The project includes managing invasive species—the familiar privet and bush honeysuckle—and stabilizing the stream bank by planting warm season grasses and container-grown native trees and shrubs. This reduces erosion and enhances the stream corridor as wildlife habitat. There have been some modifications in the streambed itself that enhance the habitat for the endangered Nashville crayfish, and there is a wetland along the trail between it and Edmondson Pike.

Rivers and Streams

Accounts of the early explorers and hunters who came to what is today's Nashville told of a place that was "well watered." Nashville is indeed blessed with an abundance of water in the form of a major river, the Cumberland; lengths of two of it major tributaries, the Stones and the Harpeth; big creeks such as Mill and Whites; and smaller streams such as Browns, Richland, Seven-Mile, and Vaughn Creeks. Modern dams have created three big reservoirs, Cheatham and Old Hickory on the Cumberland River, and J. Percy Priest on the Stones River. Today, 4.5% of Davidson County's surface is water.

Given the Nashville area's degree of development and unplanned sprawl, it should not be surprising that some of Nashville's water is impaired. Sections of most every waterway in Davidson County suffer some form of degradation from storm water runoff, sewer and pump station overflows, or habitat degradation.

Increased public awareness and concern for water quality are assisting regulators end these impairments, and water quality is better now that it once was. As an example, in recent years there has been a 94% reduction in pump station overflows. Conditions have improved on the Cumberland River to such an extent that the Music City Triathlon has held its swimming competition downtown on the river. Time will tell whether Nashville continues to make the improvements necessary to return all segments of the rivers and streams to their healthy condition.

Long-range plans call for the Seven Mile Creek Greenway to extend upstream to the Edmonson Pike branch of the Nashville Public Library.

In addition to the Metro Parks greenway, downstream there is a small privately owned and maintained greenway segment where Harding Place (TN 255) crosses the creek by the Wal-Mart.

ELLINGTON AGRICULTURAL CENTER

Brief Description: *Former estate with forest, fields, and streams*
Location: *Crieve Hall: off Edmonson Pike or Hogan Road*
Facilities: *Hiking trails*
Management: *Tennessee Department of Agriculture*

Area Description

The Ellington Agricultural Center is a 207-acre green oasis on the eastern edge of the Crieve Hall neighborhood. The grounds surround the 1927 baronial mansion of financier Rogers Caldwell that came into state ownership following the collapse of his banking empire in the Great Depression. The center, named for the late Governor Buford Ellington, houses a variety of state government functions including the agriculture department and the wildlife resources agency as well as the stable for Nashville's mounted police. The center is also home to the Farris Agricultural Museum and the Middle Tennessee Iris Society Garden. The iris is Tennessee's state flower.

Ellington's landscape consists of a combination of Seven Mile Creek, manicured lawns, open fields, successional forest, and a climax forest holding some exceptionally large trees. This patch of woods holds a nice collection of spring-blooming trillium. Biologists have identified sixty-nine different tree species on the estate.

The center's grounds can be enjoyed on 2.2 miles of unpaved trail and on the center's paved roads. Rogers' Walk circles the grounds for 1.6 miles and passes though the variety of habitats. There are trailheads at both the Hogan Road and Edmondson Pike entrances.

Much of the walking is along Seven Mile Creek and a small tributary, Briarwood Branch, which the State is restoring to their natural riparian environments. The effort shows how even a waterway through a highly developed urban environment can be managed to nurture its natural features (see also the Seven Mile Creek Greenway above.) The Rogers' Walk trail also passes through a ten-acre field being maintained in its open state for wildlife habitat. It is a nice place to see summer wildflowers. If it were not mowed now and then, it would eventually revert to forest.

WHITES CREEK GREENWAY

Brief Description: Linear park along a major Cumberland River tributary
Location: Bordeaux and Whites Creek: off Tucker Road at Hartman Park or Clarksville Pike (US 41A) and off Whites Creek Pike (US 431)
Facilities: Paved trail, hiking trail, canoe access, restrooms at Hartman Park
Management: Metro Parks

Area Description

Whites Creek is the longest stream wholly within Davidson County, and plans call for a greenway to follow the creek twenty-six miles from its headwaters to its ecologically rich mouth at the Cumberland River. As of this writing, there is a one-mile greenway segment open in Bordeaux from Hartman Park on Tucker Road to Clarksville Pike (US 41A) and trails at Fontanel, the former estate at Whites Creek that is now a popular dining and entertainment destination.

The Bordeaux section follows the banks of the broad, sycamore-lined creek past an island that has not been bothered in many years. It harbors a row of huge trees, including cherry, northern red oak, walnut, and box elder. The trail gently climbs up the side of a steep ridge populated with a stately stand of older hardwoods where woodpeckers are often heard pounding away. Plentiful spring wildflowers in this area include spring beauty, trout lily, Solomon's seal, Jack-in-the-pulpit, cut-leaf toothwort, bloodroot, and May apple. It is not unusual to find deer along this greenway, and great blue heron can be spotted prowling the creek in search of prey.

Plans call for an extension of the greenway up Clarksville Pike to the Bordeaux Branch of the Nashville Public Library.

Whites Creek Greenway

The segment downstream from Clarksville Pike is slated for construction next and will include thirty-acre Mullins Park. At the urging of Bordeaux residents, Metro Parks in 2009 acquired the land where the creek passes under Ashland City Highway (TN 12). The park will be named for Joseph Brown Mullins, a successful, multifaceted black businessman who in the early twentieth century began developing housing in Bordeaux.

Near the headwaters of Whites Creek, Metro Parks has partnered with Fontanel to provide access to 2.5 miles of trail on the 136 acres of pristine woods around the massive log home. It was built for entertainer Barbara Mandrell and husband Ken Dudney, and the estate now houses a popular outdoor music venue, Woods Amphitheater, and a fine restaurant in addition to the trails.

Whites Creek and the nearby community get their name from Zachariah White, one of Nashville's original settlers, who was killed in the 1781 Battle of the Bluff at Fort Nashborough.

CENTENNIAL PARK

Brief Description: *Developed urban park*
Location: *West End: off West End Avenue*
Facilities: *Paved trail, The Parthenon, restrooms*
Management: *Metro Parks*

Area Description

Centennial Park is the crown jewel of Nashville's park system. It spreads over 132-acres off West End Avenue a few miles from downtown near Vanderbilt University. Because it has been in public protection since 1901, it has some uncommonly large trees. Metro Parks has published a guide to the Centennial Park Tree Tour that shows the location of seventy-eight species, both such natives as several kinds of oak, tulip poplar, beech, black walnut, sycamore, and sugar maple, as well as such non-natives as Chinese pistacia, panicled golden raintree, Persian ironwood, and English oak.

The trees can be visited from the one-mile paved trail that circles the interior of the park. The trail also passes the sunken garden, band shell, and Lake Watauga, named for the Upper East Tennessee river where in the mid-1700s the first European and African-American settlement of what is now Tennessee took place. The original settlers who arrived at today's Nashville in 1779-80 came mostly from the Watauga area.

The centerpiece of Centennial Park is the Parthenon, an exact replica of the original in ancient Greece, reflecting that Nashville is known as the "Athens of the South." Centennial Park and the Parthenon owe their existence to the Tennessee

Centennial Exposition held on this site in 1897, a year late, to mark the 100th anniversary of Tennessee's admission to the Union in 1796. The Parthenon replica built for the exposition was intended to be permanent, but it did not hold up well, so it was replaced in the 1920s. It is now an important art center.

The Parthenon in Centennial Park

When the exposition closed, the decision was made to convert the grounds to a public park, and the Nashville parks department was created in 1901 for that purpose. Stimulated by the support group Conservancy for the Parthenon & Centennial Park, a new master plan has been created, that when implemented will make the park even more pedestrian-friendly.

RICHLAND CREEK GREENWAY

Brief Description: Linear park near an urban stream
Location: Sylvan Park and The Nations: off Harding Road (US 70S), Cherokee Road, Wyoming Avenue, White Bridge Road, and Urbandale Avenue
Facilities: Paved trail, connections to trailheads, restrooms at McCabe Park
Management: Metro Parks

Area Description

The Richland Creek Greenway runs along the recovering urban stream in Sylvan Park and The Nations offering a splendid outdoor experience for a wide section of the western part of Nashville.

The Sylvan Park section circles the twenty-seven-hole McCabe Park golf course and runs along the wooded banks of Richland Creek for about a mile. With connections to trailheads and stretches away from the creek, the length is four miles. The greenway does not quite make a complete loop, so until a short segment is built past the golf course club house, greenway users must navigate the parking lot. A nice aspect of this greenway is that it provides a pedestrian and bicycle link between several residential neighborhoods and the commercial areas on Harding (US 70S) and White Bridge (TN 155) Roads.

Richland Creek Greenway

Only the railroad tracks separate McCabe Park and the greenway from the ninety-two-acre Dominican Campus that is home to three schools. The National Wildlife Federation has certified the campus as an official wildlife habitat, and the combination of park, greenway, and campus keeps forever green a huge swath of urban Nashville.

Richland Creek is a magnet for water-loving birds, so visitors can expect to see duck, Canada geese, kingfisher, and Tennessee's largest nesting bird, the great blue heron. Keep an eye out for other birds as well, such as several species of owl and woodpecker, plus such common species as robin, cardinal, and blue jay. There have even been sightings of wild turkey along the creek.

Several species of oak populate the woods that protect the creek by McCabe Park, including several large black oak and burr oak. Other trees are black locust, tulip poplar, black cherry, sassafras, butternut hickory, and Osage orange. The blooms on the vines of Virginia creeper and trumpet creeper brighten up the area, as do several species of native wildflowers. Sections of the greenway have been planted with a non-native wildflower mix that includes primrose, crown and smooth vetch, and orange and purple mustard. The usual suspects of non-native pests, bush honeysuckle and privet, have invaded Richland Creek.

Snakes

Though the presence of snakes is evidence of a healthy ecosystem, the creatures do not get the respect they deserve as an integral part of the natural environment. Only three of the twenty or so species found in Middle Tennessee are venomous, but nevertheless many people are afraid of all snakes.

One interesting feature of snakes is that they molt, shedding their skin several times a year. It is not uncommon to find on the ground the intact skin of an entire snake. Rattlesnakes get new rattles with each molting. The timber rattlesnake is one of the venomous snakes. Copperhead and cottonmouth are the others. Venomous snakes are most easily recognized by their triangular-shaped heads that are wider than their bodies. The heads of the other species are about the same width as their necks.

Snakes are afraid of people, and most often flee when humans are around, so if there is one is in the area where you are, more than likely it will have hidden. If you do see one, enjoy it at a safe distance. You may not want to get close enough to inspect its head to see if it is venomous or harmless. In truth, though, snakebites are quite rare.

The Sylvan Park section's interpretative signs have a transportation theme. McCabe Park covers the site of McConnell Field, Nashville's first official airport that operated from 1927 to 1937. The rail line was built in the 1850s, and the original pre-Civil War limestone pilings stand next to the newer bridge. The deadliest train wreck in U.S. history occurred here in 1918 during World War I when two trains collided head-on on Dutchman's Curve, killing more than 100 people.

The original bridge that gives White Bridge Road its name now carries a greenway spur from the Hill Center over the creek and tracks. Completed in 1913, the 512-foot bridge is an early example of concrete T-beam that replaced iron truss as the dominant form of bridge construction. Howard M. Jones designed the bridge, as he did the acclaimed Shelby Street Bridge across the Cumberland River downtown.

Richland Creek Greenway

Downstream from Charlotte Avenue (US 70) in the neighborhood known as The Nations, a park has been established where houses stood before the 2010 floods, and a greenway segment runs through the park and upstream to the police precinct station on Charlotte. The park is named for Andrew and Martha England, who lost their lives in the flood one year before their sixtieth wedding anniversary.

Nashville founder James Robertson is responsible for the creek's name. He and his wife, Charlotte, a powerful force in her own right, established their permanent home in 1784 on a farm that was along the creek near today's England Park.

RADNOR LAKE STATE NATURAL AREA

Brief Description: *Forested ridges and coves around an eighty-acre lake*

Location: *Oak Hill: Otter Creek Road between Granny White Pike and Franklin Road (US 31)*

Facilities: *Paved trail, hiking trails, wildlife observation sites, visitor center, restrooms*

Management: *State Parks*

Area Description

Radnor's 1,258 acres of near-wilderness just seven miles from downtown Nashville take in most of the basin of the headwaters of Otter Creek. The preserve features an eighty-acre lake, placid sloughs, creeks, grown up fields, and a dense older forest. Elevations range from 774 to 1,160 feet, the highest point in Davidson County. Radnor's diverse ecological system is home to five distinct plant communities, eighteen species of mammals, seventeen species of reptiles, and several species of amphibians. The dry ridgetops are home to mountain laurel, blueberry, oak, and hickory, while the lower elevations are covered with sugar maple, tulip poplar, and shagbark hickory and an understory of spicebush, coralberry, and elderberry.

More than 250 bird species have been observed at Radnor. The lake is a haven for waterfowl, with twenty-two species making this their winter home. Ducks encountered in the winter include ring-neck duck, lesser scaup, canvasback, bufflehead, gadwall, and American widgeon. Coots are abundant as well. Wood duck, mallards, and Canada geese nest at Radnor Lake. Members of the Tennessee Ornithological Society report daily sightings of more than twenty-five species of warblers during spring and fall migrations, and in recent years, bald eagles have been spending parts of their summers at Radnor.

Beginning with the spring beauty that covers the hillsides sometimes as early as February, some of the 325 kinds of flowering plants are blooming all year except in the dead of winter.

Otter have returned to Radnor Lake

The well-maintained network of hiking trails skirts the lake, penetrates the hollows, and crests the ridges. Trailheads are at both the east and west entrances. The stretch of paved Otter Creek Road along the lake is closed to motor vehicles, which makes it an ideal place for the disabled and walkers looking for a more stable surface. Some of the best views of the lake and its waterfowl are from this mile-long part of the road.

An easy loop walk of 3.3 miles combines the Spillway, Lake, and South Lake trails and stretches of Otter Creek Road. A more demanding hike that takes in the tops of the tall ridges uses stretches of those trails plus the Ganier Ridge and South Cove Trails, for a total length of 4.5 miles.

The lake is not open to private boats, but the park's staff periodically hosts canoe floats. The full-moon floats are particularly popular. The visitor center at the west entrance houses exhibits on the natural and human history of the area, and visitors can get more information about Radnor and find out about the abundant naturalist-led activities. The center is named for Walter Criley who served as State Parks planning director when Radnor Lake was established as a state preserve.

The lake is created by a dam completed in 1914 to provide water for the Louisville & Nashville Railroad yard over the hills from the Otter Creek Basin, and it was not long before the lake became a haven for migratory waterfowl and other birds. A founder of the Tennessee Ornithological Society, Albert F. Ganier, and a railroad man himself as well as a serious amateur naturalist and historian, in 1923 persuaded the L&N to designate the area as a wildlife sanctuary. As Nashville grew around it, the Otter Creek Basin remained in its natural state.

The demise of steam locomotives eliminated the railroad's need for the lake, so in 1962 the L&N sold the property. When it looked like the basin was going to be carved up into lots, a massive grassroots effort to save Radnor proved successful, and Radnor Lake became the first area acquired under Tennessee's Natural Areas Preservation Act of 1971. Over the years, and with the help of Friends of Radnor Lake,

The Nature Conservancy, and The Land Trust for Tennessee, the protected area has expanded from its original 747 acres to its current size, and more additions are planned when funding is secured. The preserve now receives more visitors than any unit of Tennessee's state park system.

Like so many of the places in Middle Tennessee, Radnor traces its name to a place of origin of settlers who migrated west from the original thirteen states. The name of the lake comes from the railroad yard that still hums with activity just over the ridge. The yard in turn takes its name from the part of town where it is located, which in turn takes its name from an early school named "Radnor," which in turn takes its name from Radnor, Pennsylvania, hometown of the school's founder.

Solitude at Radnor Lake and the Warner Parks
Carol Rehder

Hiking with my friends at Radnor and Warner Parks gives me immense pleasure and opportunity to strengthen those relationships, but my solitary journeys in these natural places touch my heart.

I take advantage of entering these spots when fewer people are around, allowing the rhythm of these areas to speak their voice. It's really a conversation where these places listen to my feelings of joy and thankfulness as well as my tears of sorrow and grief, and I listen for their lessons. These natural settings first received the deeper story of change after my husband died. I always leave feeling embraced by the comfort of healing and knowing I am not alone.

At Radnor I remember as I walk the Lake Trail that my mother and step-father who married in their very late seventies grew their love walking these paths. One day a ranger appeared at their nearby home with a box of strawberries because he had missed seeing them for a couple of weeks. On Ganier Ridge I frequently walk under two trees I have named the groaning trees. When the wind catches their slender trunks, they rub against each other releasing their sounds of intimacy.

There is a bench on the South Cove Trail I have claimed as my own where I often sit and journal and I love the familiarity of my view from that bench. Twice in recent years on this trail, I have been present at the very moment spring rushed in with its overwhelming, chaotic excitement and symphony of birth, explosion of wild flower color and heady perfume with its promise of new beginnings. Being present during the release of this energy makes me dizzy with its pleasure. In the fall, I have heard the sounds of mating deer and stood in awe at the winter beauty of sunlight on thousands of ice crystals.

Sometimes I find more privacy on the Warner Parks trails, especially the Mossy Ridge Trail. I like to say my prayers out loud, and this trail extends that invitation to me. More than once I have rounded a curve seeing another hiker who appears to wonder if a wild woman is being encountered. What better place to utter wild prayers.

I know I am a guest in these natural places, and I think of them as friends—both tender and fierce. If I am open to their surprise, they reveal their deepest gifts. My heart is grateful to those who made these places possible and to those who nurture them now.

Carol Rehder served on the staff of The Land Trust for Tennessee.

WARNER PARKS

Brief Description: Forested hills, fields, seasonal waterfalls, Little Harpeth River, and Willow Pond

Location: Between Belle Meade and Bellevue: end of Belle Meade Boulevard, off Highway 100, and Vaughn Road

Facilities: Paved trails, hiking trails, bridle paths, mountain bike trail, nature center, restrooms

Management: Metro Parks

Area Description

The twin parks in the Harpeth Hills named for brothers Percy and Edwin Warner comprise 3,138 acres of meadows, deep woods, successional habitats, a patch of old growth forest, a stretch of the Little Harpeth River, smaller streams, wet weather springs and waterfalls, and Willow Pond. Percy Warner Park is east of Old Hickory Boulevard (TN 254) and Edwin Warner Park is to the west, but the two are managed as a single unit, forming one of the nation's largest and most appealing urban parks. Most of the parks' forested portions are designated as state natural areas, and the entire parks are on the National Register of Historic Places.

The Warner Parks are noted for their wildflowers, as they harbor an amazing 400-plus species of blooming plants. Something is blooming almost year-round. Spring is particularly beautiful, when a stroll along a road or trail yields one species after another. Any time of the year visitors will likely encounter several of the thirty species of mammals and some of the nearly 200 species of birds. The parks are noted for their population of bluebirds partly due to the work ornithologist Amelia Laskey started in 1936 and continued until her death in 1973.

Because of the transitional nature of the western mesophytic forest, comprising elements of woods in both the Central Basin and on the Western Highland Rim, the forest diversity is staggering: 133 kinds of trees, shrubs, and woody vines. This includes twelve species of oak, six species of hickory, and five species of maple. Massive beech trees populate some of the hollows.

Most hiking trails can be reached from the Deep Well entrance off Highway 100 in Percy Warner Park and the Nature Center west of the Old Hickory Boulevard intersection in Edwin Warner Park. The Warner Parks trails lead to such inviting places Dripping Springs, a seasonal waterfall, Phlox Hollow, Quiet Point, Trillium Curve, and Larkspur Hill.

The Deep Well trailhead is the beginning for both the 2.5-mile Warner Woods Trail and the 4.5-mile Mossy Ridge Trail that combine to form a giant figure eight. The 2.4-mile Harpeth Woods Trail in Edwin Warner Park can be accessed at the Nature Center where there are also short nature trails. The 1.0-mile Cane Connector links the Mossy Ridge Trail to the Nature Center, making it possible to combine all three loop trails for a more ambitious hike of nearly 10 miles. The short Owl Hollow Trail loops from the road on the backside of Edwin Warner Park near the picnic areas reached from Vaughn Road. Owls are most likely to be spotted at dawn and dusk.

The parks have some "tree trails" where numbers on trees correspond to a brochure that identifies different species and tells a little about them, such as common uses for their wood.

Warner Parks

Walkers, runners, and cyclists as well as motor vehicles use the twenty-eight miles of scenic roads that twist and turn through the parks, taking advantage of the land's natural contours to reinforce the feeling of solitude. In Edwin Warner Park, seven miles of paved road are closed to motor vehicles, making them popular for walkers and runners and suitable for baby strollers and use by the disabled.

Percy Warner Park's eighteen miles of bridle paths provide one of the few places in Middle Tennessee for horseback riding on public land. The Equestrian Center and bridle path trailhead are off Old Hickory Boulevard just east of the steeplechase course.

The Warner Parks bridle paths, hiking trails, and roads never seem crowded, even when activity is at its heaviest; that is, except for the second Saturday in May when the Iroquois Steeplechase is run on the beautiful course. Thousands pack the place to party to the sound of thundering thoroughbreds at one of the world's major events for the sport.

The parks' man-made environment competes for beauty with the natural one. Using native materials, the WPA, the 1930s Depression-era public works agency, built seven limestone entrances, two stone bridges, miles of dry-stacked stone walls, the steeplechase course, bridle paths, and picnic areas. The formal entrance at the end of Belle Meade Boulevard is constructed of smooth-dressed Sewanee sandstone and topped with stone eagles. Behind it a less formal 875-foot stair-step lane provides a transition from the formal entrance into the woods.

The Warner Parks Nature Center near the Highway 100-Old Hickory Boulevard intersection is a great place to start any visit. The center hosts a year-round schedule of activities for people of all ages, including school programs coordinated with Nashville's schools that serve 10,000 children each year. On the Nature Center grounds there is a trailhead, library, gardens, native landscaping, pond and wetland, natural play area, and the Suzanne Warner Bass Learning Center. This remarkable structure is named for Edwin Warner's daughter (1910-2000), whose family continues to support the parks in a variety of ways. It has permanent exhibits, and the building itself is of interest. It was built using materials salvaged from other structures and has a permanent display of nineteen works of art. Its 5,000-square-foot interior is surrounded by 2,500 square feet of porches. The nature center was built by funds raised by the Friends of Warner Parks.

Nature study at the Warner Parks Nature Center

Percy Warner (1861-1927), for whom one of the parks is named, was a prosperous electric utility pioneer who since his youth had been a lover of nature and the outdoors. As chairman of the Nashville Parks Board in the 1920s, he envisioned a necklace of green parks around the city connected by scenic boulevards. At the same time, his son-in-law, the indefatigable Luke Lea, was developing Belle Meade Plantation into a fashionable neighborhood. Warner in 1927 convinced Lee to donate the parks' original 868 acres at the end of Belle Meade Boulevard. Warner took a personal interest in the park and designed much of the scenic road network, but a heart attack unexpectedly claimed his life the following year. Edwin Warner (1871-1945) succeeded his brother as parks board chairman, a position he held until 1945. It was under Edwin's leadership that the park expanded west of Old Hickory Boulevard.

Much of the rugged terrain north of the Warner Parks between Highways 100 and 70S remained undeveloped as development spread around the parks. Through several purchases, Friends of Warner Parks acquired 424 acres to extend parkland over the ridges to Highway 70S. The addition will connect to Edwin Warner Park via a tunnel under Highway 100 and the busy railroad track. Most of the land north of Highway 100 is called the Burch Reserve in honor of the family of Lucius E. Burch, III, who provided much of the funding.

The most dramatic part of the northward expansion is the 225-acre old growth forest that is part of the larger Hill Tract acquired by the friends group. Old growth (see p. 11) is rare in the eastern United States and nearly unheard of in urban areas. Among the giant oak, hickory, and maple are trees more than 200 years old. The tract gets its name from grocery magnate H. G. Hill (1873-1942), who acquired the land intending to make it his home, but never did. Ownership passed to the H. G. Hill Realty Company, a major Nashville landowner and developer that sold the tract to Friends at a heavy discount from its appraised value. The old growth forest is an officially designated state natural area, and access to it is limited to guided tours.

Bordering Percy Warner Park near the Belle Meade Boulevard entrance is Cheekwood. Cheekwood is a fifty-five-acre estate that includes the fine arts center housed in the glorious Georgian Revival mansion built by Leslie Cheek, who made a fortune in Maxwell House Coffee, and his wife, Mabel Wood Cheek. (Cheekwood is a combination of their names.) Completed in 1932, the house was designed by one of the nation's leading architects, Bryant Fleming of New York, the same person who designed the Belle Meade Boulevard entrance to Percy Warner Park. The Cheeks' daughter, Huldah Cheek Sharp, in the 1950s offered the site to the public for a museum and gardens.

In addition to being a major center for the visual arts, Cheekwood is a first-class botanical garden. Highlights for nature lovers are the Cora B. Howe Wildflower Garden, the

Wills Perennial Garden, and the mile-long Carell Woodland Sculpture Trail. The wildflower garden was started by Howe at her East Nashville home and relocated to Cheekwood in 1968. The Wills Garden hosts a number of nectoring butterflies, especially in the summer and fall. The sculpture trail is a stunning blend of art and nature, where world-class sculpture is scattered in a forest that has been cleared of the invasive, non-native species that are causing such a problem in the adjacent park. There is an admission charge to Cheekwood.

The Seasons at the Warner Parks
Deb Beazley

One of the best things about living in Nashville is having the opportunity to experience four distinct seasons, and for me, nothing compares to the seasonal wonders in the Warner Parks.

Every spring I say that this MUST be my favorite season. Walking the Mossy Ridge Trail from Deep Well to Gum Ridge in early spring is both overwhelming and rejuvenating. Being surrounded by a multi-colored carpet of flowers like trilliums, trout lilies, Dutchman's breeches, larkspur, phacelia, and may apples, to name a few, is awesome! The wet weather springs are flowing, pawpaw flowers dangle overhead, spicebush blossoms are everywhere, and I love the huge, red bud scales from the shagbark hickories littering the trail. Fern fiddleheads are pushing through the leaf litter. All the while cardinals, titmice, chickadees, woodpeckers, and wrens fill the woods with music. Everyone is happy! Then, I can't wait to explore the pond at the Nature Center to witness the toad orgy resulting in thousands of egg strands strewn like black necklaces all over the wetland, while the garter snakes emerge from slumber in the wildflower garden all entangled like knotted ropes.

Every fall I say that this MUST be my favorite season. Walking the Meadow Tree Trail in Edwin Warner is a fantastic opportunity to become submerged in a sea of asters, frostweed, goldenrod, black-eyed-Susans, ironweed, milkweeds and all the zillions of insects going about their busy business. With over 100 species of trees, fall colors are brilliant throughout the Parks. One of my favorite trees is the big sassafras by the cross country track parking lot on Highway 100, which turns a deep orange color. A real treat is walking the Tornado Road section of Mossy Ridge where the black gums, sourwoods, hickories and oaks put on a blazing show of bright reds and yellows all over the ridge top.

I have grown to love winter in the Warner Parks. Along every trail or road throughout the woods, I find the scattered, subtle hues absolutely lovely. Crossvine dangling from naked branches like tiny magenta and green drapes is especially nice, while the wild grapevines twist and turn all over the trees. The moss-covered limestone outcroppings are a park trademark, along with the many smooth, gray beech trees each with its own distinctive silhouette. I always pause by one and look for barred owls, or any number of critters that love to hide in the many knot holes. A true winter wonder is frostweed. Beginning in November and for several months this plant exudes frozen sap from the base of the dead stem. The best place to see a lot of these miniature ice palaces is just beyond the first four-way stop at the Chickering Road entrance. Throughout winter I am especially on the lookout for deer and coyote when they can't so easily hide in the leafless woods.

Finally there is summer, which can be hot, humid, and full of ticks and chiggers. The naturalist in me really comes out now because I enjoy and appreciate many of the wonders of summer. Finding that first rare, huge, green hickory horned devil caterpillar touting its burnt orange spiny "antlers" is simply awesome. I often stand along the Little Harpeth near the neat octagonal shelter enjoying the longnose gars that like to float lazily like sticks in the deep water. The Nature Center gardens are wonderfully full of flowers, toads, praying mantis, tortoise beetles, assassin bugs, spiders, butterflies, caterpillars, and hummingbirds. This is the best place to see beautiful cross vines and passion flowers blooming.

No season is complete without taking a moment to watch the bluebirds. With 75 nesting boxes scattered throughout the Warner Parks there are plenty of opportunities to enjoy this absolutely gorgeous bird who carries with it all the seasons; the bright blue spring sky, the snow white of winter, the russet orange of fall, and most likely hunting the many grasshoppers of summer. Warner Parks are wonderful in every season.

Deb Beazley is a naturalist at the Warner Parks Nature Center.

Night Owls at the Warner Parks
Bob English

The group of campers standing before me looked distracted as I talked about owls. This was my last group of the night, and it looked like it would be a tough job to keep their interest. There was a lot of talking, a lot of flirting. And why not? It was a beautiful night to be outside. We were doing programs for the PEN (People Exploring Nature) Pals.

The campers from the Nashville community centers were split into 5 or 6 groups, so that each group rotated through the various programs. But this would be the toughest group, I thought. As I talked about owls, I got the distinct impression that not a word was getting through. We started our night hike and I stopped to voice-call a barred owl. The memory phrase is, "Who cooks for you, who cooks for you-all," I told them (a few giggles from the back). I called a couple of times—no response. The group was trying to be polite, but you could tell they were having a hard time holding back the laughter. The call does sound pretty strange.

Then it happened. Suddenly, directly in front of us, there was the flash of great wings as a barred owl pulled up sharply to land on the branch of an oak tree not forty feet away! The reaction was immediate—the whole group collectively took a step, stumbled *really, backwards. There were audible gasps. Eyes were wide, mouths dropped open. The owl fixed us with fierce dark eyes for a moment. Then, just as suddenly as it appeared, it was gone. Later, after the night hike was done and the group drifted away, I took a minute to relax and look up at the sky. They won't remember me, I thought, and they won't remember anything I said tonight. But you know what? They'll remember that owl.*

_____

Bob English is an environmental educator.

Bicycling in the Warner Parks
John Norris

It's twenty-four degrees, my water bottle is frozen solid, and I'm at risk of being passed by runners as I climb nine-mile hill, but I have a smile on my face because the Warner Parks in the winter are so beautiful from a bicycle. They are also gorgeous in the spring, summer, and fall. Bicycling in the Warner Parks can be brutally difficult or leisurely, depending on your fitness level, gearing, and pace, but it is always uplifting.

If you want a scenic challenge, ride the full 11.2-mile course in Percy Warner Park. Start at the Belle Meade Boulevard entrance to Percy Warner Park and bear right.

Enjoy the flat and downhill sections because the hills will make you work. The course starts with two short but steep climbs, and the hill that crests just past the three-mile marker borders on punishing. As you pass an entrance to Harpeth Hills Golf Course more than six miles into the ride, there is a very steep downhill (watch out for deer at the bottom) followed by an equally steep uphill. And unless you bail out before then, you will soon find yourself on the final climb after making a sharp right turn. While all the descents must be made with care, the last mile contains two hairpin turns that require considerable slowing.

Be careful but enjoy the experience. Once you pass the half-mile marker and then the fork that leads back down to the entrance, you are truly in deep woods. You will see trees, big trees—oaks, beeches, and tulip poplars to name a few. It's a tossup whether the beech trees, gray with smooth bark or the tall and straight tulip poplars are more striking. And the oaks are majestic. Past the two mile marker and then the Indian Springs trailhead is a tulip poplar on the left with a diameter of close to six feet. It's one of the largest trees in Davidson County.

If you ride in the Warner Parks enough, you will see an amazing variety of wildlife for a major metropolitan area. Deer and turkey are abundant and are frequently spotted, especially in the early morning and at dusk. Other large birds include pileated woodpeckers, barred and great horned owls, hawks, and vultures. In addition to deer, commonly seen mammals are squirrels, chipmunks, raccoons, possums, foxes, skunks, groundhogs, rabbits, and, for better or worse, coyotes. If you are lucky, you might even come across a bobcat.

My all-time favorite encounter was with a timber rattlesnake. After I nudged its tail in an effort to get it off the road so it would not be run over by a car, the snake coiled and rattled spectacularly. Transfixed, I watched for what seemed like a long time and then, after a car approached, swept the snake off the road with a branch. It soon disappeared in the underbrush but not from my memory.

Rock walls, built by WPA workers in the 1930s, parallel the road for much of the ride. Whatever the fairness of having public employees work on a park to which there was no access by public transportation, the walls are handsome and provide protection from erosion. And lizards and snakes love them. Keep an eye out for rat and garter snakes as well as skinks in and around the walls, especially when the sun is shining.

The Warner Parks are plenty hilly, and bicycling up and down them does wonders for your heart and lungs. But it does even *more for your psyche. Tension melts away with the miles, and the hassles of life in the twenty-first century are put into perspective. No matter how much is wrong with most of the world, this little corner of it feels nearly perfect.*

John Norris served as Chairman of the Metro Parks Greenways Commission and President of Greenways for Nashville.

HARPETH RIVER

Brief Description: Sections of linear park and canoe access on a designated scenic river
Location: Bellevue and Newsom Station: off Highway 100, US 70S, Harpeth Bend Drive, Old Harding Road, Coley Davis Road, Newsom Station Road, and McCrory Lane
Facilities: Paved trails, hiking trails, canoe access
Management: Metro Parks and State Parks

Area Description

The Harpeth River is one of the loveliest pastoral streams in the United States. Along its 125-mile run from Mount Vernon Spring southwest of Murfreesboro to the Cumberland River near Ashland City, it graces Nashville with its presence for about fifteen miles. And even though the Harpeth in Davidson County winds through highly developed and ever-growing Bellevue, the river maintains its near-pristine character. The Davidson County stretch is a designated state scenic river. The Harpeth River's abundance of wildlife, fascinating historic sites, gentle grade, and easy access account for why the river is a magnet for anyone seeking a quiet outdoor experience and for why it is designated a "blueway."

Blueways

A "blueway" is a route along a floatable waterway with strategically located public access points. Like a greenway, a blueway is formally designated, named, and maintained. The Tennessee Scenic Rivers Association (TSRA) has studied Nashville's waterways and concluded that the Cumberland, Harpeth, and Stones Rivers, as well as Mill Creek, are suitable for designation as blueways. There are some but not enough access points on each of them. The TSRA has identified additional locations and is working with the management agencies to have them opened. The Harpeth River is the first officially designated blueway in Davidson County.

Both Metro Parks and State Parks welcome visitors to the Harpeth. As envisioned, the Metro Parks greenway will extend the river's entire length in Davidson County. Several segments are open as of this writing.

The longest starts near the Nature Center in Edwin Warner Park. It follows old Hicks Road past Ensworth High School on the site of Devon Farm with its extant 1796 house, meets the Little Harpeth River and follows it to its mouth at the Big Harpeth River and follows the Harpeth into Bellevue, a distance of 2.1 miles. A short connector links the riverside greenway to the Exchange Club ball fields off Harpeth Bend Road. The greenway continues 2.5 miles to Old Harding Road then parallels Morton Mill Road for another 2.0 miles.

There are two segments off Coley Davis Road west of the US 70S-I-40 junction. The first is a half-mile loop at Harpeth River Park in a river bend accessible by a bridge from the Harpeth Youth Soccer Association fields, and the second is a

.64 mile segment in the Harpeth Springs development farther out Coley Davis Road.

The final completed segment is off Newsom Station Road in the River Walk residential development. The developers not only included the greenway in their construction, they named the neighborhood after the 1.5-mile greenway section.

There are three units of the Harpeth River State Park in Davidson County: a canoe access on the west end of the Highway 100 bridge, Newsom's Mill, and Hidden Lake. Newsom's Mill includes the substantial remains of a mill house constructed of huge slabs of dressed limestone that were quarried nearby. The Newsom family came to this area around 1800, and from then on, there has been a mill at this site. The remains visible today were erected in 1862. The concrete dam dates to 1907.

The Hidden Lake unit of the state park rests where the Harpeth starts to leave the Outer Central Basin and cut its way through the Western Highland Rim. This intersection of two ecoregions plus the river and two ponds offer a rich diversity of habitat. A trail of about a mile meanders through the successional forest starting at the wildflower-filled field off McCrory Lane. Typical summer flowers are ironweed and black-eyed Susan. This is a popular place for observing butterflies.

The woods at Hidden Lake offer a fine display of trillium, carrion flower, pawpaw, and indigo bush. There is a shallow-soiled area where prickly pear cactus grows, which is reminiscent of the cedar glades at the opposite end of the county. The habitat diversity guarantees that the area is a magnet for birds. Red-shouldered hawks and wood ducks are common, as are migrants during their seasonal migrations.

The name "Hidden Lake" was applied to a resort that briefly operated on the property in the 1930s. The lake is actually an old quarry filled with water that is hidden between a tall bluff and the Harpeth River. There is a second smaller pond as well.

Under the leadership of the Tennessee Scenic Rivers Association and the Harpeth River Watershed Association, the designated blueway will extend ninety miles from downtown

Franklin to the Cumberland River. The Harpeth is rated as a Class One or least difficult river, but like all streams, it is dangerous when at flood. In Davidson County, there is access at Highway 100 (river mile 62.3), Harpeth River Park (mile 57.7), Newsom's Mill (mile 52.6), and Hidden Lake (mile 49.8). Maps and additional information can be obtained from the Harpeth River Watershed Association. *www.harpethriver.org.*

The Harpeth has something of a split personality depending on the season. It often gets out of its banks in winter and early spring, but in late summer and fall, it can be reduced to a trickle. In 2010 the gauge at Highway 100 went out 44,000 cubic feet per second and the river rose fifty-two feet above its normal level. On the other hand, between October 5 and 11, 1922, no flow at all was recorded for the river.

The name "Harpeth" is applied to all kinds of places, businesses, and institutions around Nashville, but not anywhere else. Middle Tennessee's Harpeth is the only river in the world with that name. There are several theories about the name's origin, but the most likely is found in an article in the August 23, 1714, edition of *The Spectator,* a popular London periodical edited by Joseph Addison. It features a story about two brothers, one named "Harpath" who drowned in a river forever named after him. The fact that the river is shown as "Harpath" on early maps supports this theory. In all likelihood, an explorer or early settler knew of the article or perhaps had a copy of it.

There are actually four streams in the 863-square-mile watershed that carry the name "Harpeth": the West Harpeth, the Little Harpeth, the South Harpeth, and the Big or just plain Harpeth. All but the West Harpeth have stretches on the fringe of Davidson County, and all but the South Harpeth have given their waters to the Big Harpeth before it flows through the county.

Like many Nashville neighborhoods, Bellevue takes its name from an early house. The DeMoss family built the first Belle Vue on the Harpeth around 1797.

The Harpeth: Going with the Flow
Patty Shultz

One of the best things in nature is water: looking at it, swimming in it, boating on it, and drinking it in. Our forefathers must have had similar thoughts because one of the first acts of Congress in 1787 was to declare that the rivers of this country were to be "forever free" for us, the citizens of the U.S. This right to boat the waterways has been confirmed by numerous Supreme Court cases. The original intent was for the welfare of fur traders, explorers, and early travelers, but over 200 years later that legacy is a great prize for those of us who like to paddle.

However, getting to the free-flowing waters may sometimes be a problem. You can't just cross private land, so access may be an issue. When two public ways cross, citizens have the right to get from one to the other. Because of this, bridges offer access opportunities, but there are still issues: where does one leave the car and how do you prevent erosion climbing down steep banks with your canoe or kayak?

That is why I'm part of a group affiliated with Tennessee Scenic Rivers Association that is working on establishing official access points to our rivers and streams. The idea is to have blueways: waterpaths. These are like greenways but instead of paths on land these are on the water. A goal is to see paddling access points about every five miles along Tennessee's paddle-able streams.

Locally we're working on the wonderful Harpeth River. The Narrows of the Harpeth are well known for canoeing. Here the river forms a loop; you can put your boat in, paddle about five beautiful and historically rich miles, and take out about 100 yards from where you started! Along the way you see Montgomery Bell's famous tunnel (a historic engineering feat), rocky bluffs, historic sites, rock shelters, Indian mounds, and charming Middle Tennessee countryside. But this is only five miles of the Harpeth and there are about 115 miles that can be paddled. Just think, you can step back in time traveling from the headwaters in Eagleville to where the Harpeth reaches the Cumberland River, a journey steeped in history. Along the way, the remains of mastodons have been found (as late as 1972). You can see Indian mounds, burial grounds, paintings and carvings on rocky bluffs, as well as more recent remains of early bridges and mills. There is a splendid collection of antebellum homes as well as some sturdy farmhouses from the late nineteenth and early twentieth centuries. Natural beauty is also abundant along the Harpeth. It's amazing that in our big metropolitan area, you can step away from it all, listen to the birds, and watch for wildlife and wildflowers as you meander along tree-lined banks and beneath rocky bluffs.

Wait, there's more! The Harpeth has six major tributaries. When the water level is high enough these smaller streams can be paddled and are outrageously beautiful. Let's do what we can to protect all these resources and use them with appreciation, all the while going with the flow.

Patty Shultz, author of *Paddling Around Nashville*, is active in the Tennessee Scenic Rivers Association.

Natchez Trace Parkway

Brief Description: Linear park
Location: Pasquo: off Highway 100
Facilities: Paved road, hiking trails, bridle path
Management: National Park Service

Area Description

The Natchez Trace Parkway is a 445-mile linear national park that roughly follows the path of the once-important route linking Nashville on the Cumberland River with Natchez on the Mississippi. The unit of the National Park System is home to more than 100 kinds of trees, a grand assortment of wildflowers, 215 species of birds, fifty-seven species of mammals, eighty-nine species of reptiles and amphibians, and more than sixty-six species of butterflies.

From its terminus on Highway 100 west of the Warner Parks, the parkway climbs to the heights of rugged Backbone Ridge, and twists and turns along the ridge until it descends into the headwaters of the Harpeth River near the quaint Williamson County village of Leipers Fork. The parkway is understandably popular with cyclists.

A few miles south of the Highway 100 terminus, the parkway land expands to take in a spur of Backbone Ridge. The spur ridge is covered in places with some of the biggest and oldest beech, oak, maple, hickory, and poplar trees in the Nashville area. An easy trail leads from the overlook out the ridge to the parkway boundary. The overlook is reached from a side road that runs off the Trace 2.7 miles south of Highway 100. The overlook, appropriately named the Big Tree Overlook, provides splendid views into the Harpeth River valley and the Harpeth Hills rising in the distance.

There are other walking opportunities farther down in Williamson County on the Garrison Creek Trail that begins at milepost 427.6 and extends south to the Duck River. The trail is most frequently used by horseback riders.

Coyotes

There was a time when the range of coyotes was limited to the desert Southwest, but as most everyone knows, that is no longer the case. They are now firmly established in Middle Tennessee as they are throughout much of the United States. This canine species is extraordinarily adaptable, which is one reason they thrive most anywhere. They will eat just about anything, and their sense of smell is twenty-three times stronger than humans. Coyotes have a remarkable range. Males will roam over fifteen to twenty-five square miles and females will roam over six to ten square miles. They are mostly nocturnal except during their January-March breeding session when they are more likely to be seen during the day. A typical litter will have five to six pups that are born about sixty days after breeding. Once weaned, a young coyote may travel up to 100 miles to find its own home. It is not unusual these days to hear the coyote yips, barks, and howls at night.

WESTERN HIGHLAND RIM

The Highland Rim that completely surrounds the Central Basin is in two parts, Eastern and Western, and much of northwestern Nashville-Davidson County is on the Western Highland Rim. This less-fertile upland is characterized by rolling hills dissected by numerous streams, resulting in a highly uneven terrain of forested ridges and deep narrow valleys. Stream gradients are steeper than in the Basin, and there are numerous small waterfalls where streams tumble down the escarpment. Average elevation is just less than 1,000 feet. Except where it has been cleared for agriculture or development, the Western Highland Rim is covered in a second growth forest dominated by oak and hickory.

BEAMAN PARK

Brief Description: Forested ridges and hollows, streams, and waterfalls
Location: Between Scottsboro and Joelton: off Old Hickory Boulevard and Little Marrowbone Road
Facilities: Hiking trails, nature center, restrooms
Management: Metro Parks

Area Description

This preserve protects 1,688 acres on the rugged edge of the Western Highland Rim. Ridge tops, deep hollows, pristine springs, cascading crystal clear streams, a wide variety of wildflowers, and a rich second growth forest characterize the landscape. The park is one of the most botanically diverse places in Tennessee where there are some plants more common on the Cumberland Plateau to the east and some more common to the West Tennessee lowlands. Beaman is a designated state natural area.

An oak-hickory forest dominates the higher elevations, while a more mixed forest is found along the creeks. Oak includes blackjack, northern red, scarlet, chestnut, and white. There are several kinds of hickory as well as an abundance of tulip poplar, sourwood, sassafras, redbud, and dogwood. Less common trees are Virginia and shortleaf pine, witch-hazel, Carolina willow, hazelnut, and butternut. Shrubs in the understory include spicebush, farkleberry, blueberry, wild azalea, mountain laurel, and gooseberry. One pleasing aspect of Beaman is that it has largely escaped the invasion of non-native plant species like the privet and bush honeysuckle that plague much of the rest of Davidson County.

The park staff has identified 384 kinds of wildflowers. One, Eggert's sunflower, is a federally-listed threatened species. The wildflower show is most spectacular in the spring, but it continues nearly year-round. The spring show starts with spring beauty, larkspur, wild geranium, shooting star, fire pink, and the rare lady's slipper orchid. There is no better way to experience the wildflower parade than to stroll up Henry Hollow in April beneath the canopy of bright redbud to discover one blooming plant after another.

The summer months bring out blazing star, coreopsis, New Jersey tea, bergamot, and Michigan lily, a state-listed threatened species. Fall brings blue lobelia, turtlehead, and Joe-Pye weed, beard-tongue, and ladies' tresses orchids. Much of the forest floor is covered with ferns, sedges, mosses, mushrooms, and lichens. The park is also home to an unusual landscape, a woodland barren of post oak and native grasses.

Wildlife includes mammals—deer, bobcat, fox, coyote, raccoon, fox squirrel, flying squirrel; reptiles—snakes, turtles, skinks, and lizards; and amphibians—salamanders, frogs, and toads. There are not any big fish in the streams, but there are darters, dace minnows, snails, crayfish, and aquatic insects. Birds sheltered by the deep forest include several species of woodpecker, thrush, wren, warbler, owl, and hawk.

Woodpeckers

Even if visitors do not see one of the eight species of woodpeckers that inhabit Nashville's natural areas, they are likely to hear one. Woodpeckers are "cavity nesters," which means they nest in cavities in trees, and the rapid-fire drumming sound is the bird pecking away to excavate a cavity. While it is often thought that pecking at trees is harmful to the forest, the opposite is actually true. Dead wood is softer than live wood, so the cavities they excavate are most often in dead trees or dead limbs of live trees. In addition, woodpeckers love to eat wood-boring insects that can kill trees if unchecked, so the birds help keep trees healthy by consuming the bugs.

The pileated woodpecker is the largest and easiest to spot. It has a wingspan that can measure up to thirty inches and has a bright red crest on its head. It loves the deep woods in the Warner Parks, Radnor Lake, and Beaman Park, where its loud call of "kuk-kuk-kuk" is a commonly heard.

The only one of the eight woodpecker species that is a migrant is the yellow-bellied sapsucker that visits Tennessee in the winter. Evidence of these birds is easier to spot than the birds themselves, as they like to drill rows of holes around tree trunks. They feed on the sap and on the insects that are attracted to the sap made available by the holes.

The 2.0-mile Henry Hollow Loop starts and ends at the lower parking lot off Little Marrowbone Road. The 2.1-mile Ridgetop Trail follows old logging roads along the top of one of the dry ridges and takes off from the upper parking lot off Little Marrowbone Road. It intersects with the Henry Hollow Loop. The .6-mile Sedge Hill Trail connects the nature center off Old Hickory Boulevard with the Henry Hollow Loop. Also at the nature center is a quarter-mile trail with a boardwalk suitable for use by the disabled.

Beaman Park came into being through the generosity of some doctors who once owned the land and the Beaman family who financed its purchase, as well as quick action by Mayor Phil Bredesen. Drs. John Tudor and Robert McClellan were part of Blueberry Hill Partners that had owned the land as a hunting preserve for twenty-five years. In 1996, they approached Metro Parks about selling the land for half its appraised value. When word got out that the land was available, Sally Beaman offered to donate the funds in honor of her husband, prominent businessman and civic leader, Alvin G. Beaman. Mr. Beaman had served faithfully as a member of the Nashville Parks Board from 1955 until the Metro Parks Board replaced it in 1963. Mayor Bredesen wasted no time in accepting her offer, and the acquisition became the largest single purchase in the history of Nashville's parks. The official name of the preserve is Alvin G. Beaman Park.

Beaman Park grew in size in 2007 through the generosity of Mary Proctor O'Neil and Katherine Proctor Gross. The sisters donated 188 valuable acres on Beaman's western boundary, giving the park additional frontage on Old Hickory Boulevard and a potential entrance into the remote western end of the park.

At present, the trails are limited to the northeast section of the park. There are no trails into the Big Hollow section to the west, but long-range plans call for a trail to extend through it from Old Hickory Boulevard to Little Marrowbone Road.

The early name for this part of the county, Paradise Ridge, certainly seems appropriate today, but the name actually is the last name of one-time landowners.

Beaman Park: A Humbling Experience of the Truly Awe Inspiring
Nancy Dorman

i thank You God for most this amazing
day: for the leaping greenly spirits of trees
and a blue true dream of sky; and for everything
which is natural which is infinite which is yes

—e.e. cummings

On any given day at Beaman Park the hiking trails are sprinkled with people who are not at the mall, or playing video games, or talking on their cell phone, or hurtling down the interstate at a high rate of speed. They may be a nature enthusiast or a hiker, a bird watcher or photographer, seeking the passive enjoyment of the outdoors or training for a backpacking trip, looking for solitude or the company of friends. They come for their own reasons but I wonder, what are the things that bind them together?

What is it about places like Beaman Park that draws us into a peaceful connection with nature? Is it the rugged remoteness? Is it the solitude? Is it the big trees? Is it the water? Is it the rocks? Or is it the sense of belonging that comes with an experience of the outdoors that says, "I am a part of it and it is a part of me."

For me, it is the uniqueness of each visit and the comfort of familiarity. While the experience of nature is always changing, it is the constancy of that change that is a breath of fresh air on an otherwise man-made sameness kind of day. If you spend all week sitting at a computer, hiking is a form of rest!

Many of my most powerful feelings of connectedness have come to me outdoors. When you think about it, most stories of spiritual enlightenment occurred in the outdoors: in deserts, on mountaintops, by rivers, or under a tree. Humans have frequently experienced the awe that some associate with a connection to the divine amid the beauty and wonder of the wilderness.

Beaman Park offers a chance to really slow down and notice what is around you. It is not always easy to stop our brain wheels from turning, even here in the outdoors surrounded by nature. Sometimes it takes that brush with something unexpected to force you out of your regular thoughts and into a place of attention and heightened awareness. Beaman Park provides that unique view in part because of its location on the Western Highland Rim, where many of the plants are different than those found in other Metro Parks. I hope that by noticing the little things in the world around us, we are better able to marvel at the special things we see around most every corner.

I have never been to the Grand Canyon, but I know that it has value and importance in our world and deserves the best possible care, whether I ever go there or not. I hope that when people visit Beaman Park they gain a sense the intrinsic value of wilderness like this, and are motivated to action to protect it for future generations. And, that like the snake, they feel a bit of the divine in being so close to the earth!

Nancy Dorman is a founder of Friends of Beaman Park.

ACKNOWLEDGMENTS

Shain Dennison, the Metro Parks Greenways director, and Renee Bates, Greenways for Nashville executive coordinator, provided indispensible help and ideas throughout the long life of this project. Other Metro Parks personnel who contributed were Sandy Bivens, Deb Beazley, Vera Vollbrecht, Kim Bailey, Susan Bradfield, Mark Bradfield, Denise Weyer, and Cindy Harrison. Pandy English at the Tennessee Wildlife Resources Agency provided information as well.

The maps were prepared by Carol Ashworh of Ashworth Environmental Design, Bob Firth of Informing Design, and Chris Roberts of the Land Trust for Tennessee. Most of the photographs came from Gary Layda, the ubiquitous and talented Metro Government photographer. Others were provided by Jason Allen with Friends of Long Hunter State Park, Donald Horne of Friends of Radnor Lake, Sandy Bivens and Deb Beazley at the Warner Parks Nature Center, and Wesley Aldredge.

Sharon Wiggs at Trauger & Tuke helped with word processing, Amy Lyles Wilson edited the entire manuscript, Kate Stephenson, Sandra Duncan, and Donna Nicely proofread it, and Abby Trotter and Lauren Weathers of Hall Strategies helped with the promotion.

Finally, a special thanks to the authors of the essays.

APPENDIX ONE

GETTING THERE

Maps with trailhead locations and addresses for the Metro Parks greenways can be found at www.nashville.gov/parks/greenways/. Detailed driving directions to the greenways are at *www.greenwaysfornashville.org*.

How you make your way to the greenways and parks depends on your starting point and your destination. Several greenway segments are easy to reach on foot or bicycle from nearby residential neighborhoods: Shelby Bottoms, Cumberland River, Mill Creek, Stones River, Seven Mile Creek, Whites Creek, Richland Creek, and Harpeth River. Parks easily accessible from nearby neighborhoods are Shelby, Centennial, Radnor Lake, and Percy Warner, as well as Anderson Road Recreation Area and Ellington Agriculture Center.

Segments of the Cumberland River Greenway from downtown to the edge of the Tennessee State University campus are easily accessible by workers downtown, at MetroCenter, and at the university.

Some MTA bus routes stop at or near greenways and parks, and MTA busses are equipped with racks to transport bicycles. Route 3 (West End) stops at Centennial Park and near four Richland Creek Greenway trailheads off Harding Road (US 70S) and White Bridge Road. Route 4 (Shelby) passes Shelby Park on 19th Street. Route 6 (Lebanon Road) stops by the Stones River Greenway where Lebanon Road (US 70) crosses the Stones River. Route 9 (MetroCenter) goes close to the Cumberland River Greenway's MetroCenter Levee segment. Route 10 (Charlotte) ends at Wal-Mart near the Cumberland River Brookmeade Park Greenway. Route 21 (University Connector) passes Centennial Park. Route 22 (Bordeaux) passes the Hartman Park trailhead of the Whites Creek Greenway. Route 24 (Bellevue Express) terminates near a section of the Harpeth River Greenway. Route 25 (Midtown) passes Centennial Park on 25th Avenue North. Route 38X (Antioch Express) passes Hamilton Creek Park on Bell Road and goes near Anderson Road Recreation Area. Route 72 (Edmondson Pike Connector) passes the Seven Mile Creek Greenway, Ellington Agricultural Center, and the Ezell Park trailhead on the Mill Creek Greenway. The downtown bus station, Music City Central, is only a short distance from the Cumberland River Greenway downtown segment.

Bus routes change from time to time, so for the latest information, check with the Metropolitan Transit Authority at *www.nashvillemta.org* or call 615-862-5950.

APPENDIX TWO

DEVELOPMENT OF NASHVILLE'S GREENWAYS AND NATURE PARKS

Nashville's municipal park system stems from the Tennessee Centennial Exposition that commemorated the centennial of statehood held in what is now Centennial Park a year late in 1897. (Tennessee was admitted to the Union in 1796.) The success of the exposition heightened public awareness of the value of parks, and civic leaders soon saw the opportunity to use the exposition grounds as a park. So in 1901 the city park board was created for that purpose, and to this day, Centennial remains Nashville's best-known park.

The first big step in establishing a nature park occurred in 1927 with the donation of 808 hilly acres on the edge of the residential community that was being developed on the Belle Meade Plantation. This became the nucleus of the Warner Parks that have grown to more than four times the size of the original donation. Also in the 1920s, the L&N Railroad decided to preserve as a wildlife refuge the lands around the lake it created to provide water for Radnor Yard, land that eventually became the nucleus for the Radnor Lake State Natural Area.

The Works Progress Administration (WPA) was a 1930s Great Depression-era New Deal public works agency whose activity is much in evidence in the Warner Parks. WPA workers built the stone entrance gates, stone walls, the steeplechase course, bridle paths, and picnic pavilions, as well as much of the road system. Most of the hiking trails in the Warner Parks were built in the 1970s with labor from the Youth Conservation Corps.

The Metro Parks greenways program got off to a quick start in the early 1990s and expanded to more than fifty miles by end of the first decade of the twenty-first century. The goal was to have a greenway open along each of the seven major waterways in Nashville, and that was accomplished. Linear parks continue to expand, and long-range plans call for greenways along the entire length of nearly all the major streams.

Continued development of new parks has not been limited to greenways along stream corridors. Starting in the 1990s Metro Parks in succession acquired large tracts for Shelby Bottoms, Beaman Park, Bells Bend Park, the Taylor Farm addition to Peeler Park, additions to the Warner Parks north of Highway 100, and the inclusion of the former Cornelia Fort Airpark into the Shelby Bottoms preserve.

Tennessee's state-managed parks and preserves developed in two spurts, during the New Deal of the 1930s and as part of the conservation movement in the 1960-70s. Though the WPA performed valuable work in Nashville's existing parks, none of the state parks developed by New Deal federal agencies are in Davidson County. Two are close by, Montgomery Bell in Dickson County and Cedars of Lebanon in Wilson County.

Two state laws of significance to Nashville are the Tennessee Scenic Rivers Act of 1968—the first such state law in the nation—and the Natural Areas Preservation Act of 1971. The fifteen-mile stretch of the Harpeth River winding peacefully through the county's western edge is protected as a designated scenic river by easements that preserve the river's rustic character. Radnor Lake in 1973 became the first acquisition under the state's natural areas act, and its boundary has been expanded several times.

HEROES

The biggest heroes in the development and operation of Nashville's greenways and public natural areas are the countless workers that staff the management agencies. Throughout the decades they have worked tirelessly in planning, developing, and maintaining these areas.

Here are some other heroes.

Victor Ashe. Before he was Knoxville's mayor and U.S. ambassador to Poland, he served in the Tennessee legislature where he co-sponsored the Natural Areas Preservation Act of 1971, the vehicle used to save Radnor Lake.

Warner Bass. Stalwart supporter of the Warner Parks who played a key role in most everything important that happened in the parks for several decades. Leader of expansion of the parks north of Highway 100. Edwin Warner's grandson.

Sally and Lee Beaman. Mother and son who donated funds for acquisition of 1,500 acres on the Western Highland Rim that became the park named for Alvin Beaman, Sally's husband and Lee's father, who was chair of the pre-Metro Nashville city park board.

Sandy Bivens. She began as a naturalist at the Warner Parks fresh out of college, became director of the nature center, and then led the expansion of nature centers into other parks as Metro Parks superintendent of nature centers.

Phil Bredesen. As Nashville mayor (1991-1999), he launched the Metro Parks greenways program and acquired Shelby Bottoms and Beaman Park. As Tennessee governor (2003-2011), he made land conservation a hallmark of his administration. Founded The Land Trust for Tennessee.

Bob Brown. See the dedication.

Bill Bruce. As a state senator from Memphis, he co-sponsored the 1971 Natural Areas Preservation Act that led to Radnor Lake becoming the first area acquired under the act.

Bob Clement. As Nashville's representative in the U.S. House, he secured funding for the Stones River Greenway.

Walt Criley. State Parks planning director who oversaw the implementation of the natural areas program in the 1970s and insured that resource conservation remained a mission of the State Parks. The Radnor Lake visitor center is named for him.

Karl Dean. Nashville mayor (2007—) whose commitment to open space conservation led to Nashville's first-ever open space plan and under whose administration major additions were made to the Metro Parks, including the Cornelia Fort Airpark, Hill Tract, and Taylor Farm.

Shain Dennison. Metro Parks first greenways director who skillfully implemented the greenways program.

Sandra Duncan. As a member of Mayor Bredesen's staff, she helped secure funding for a greenways staff at Metro Parks. Served on the Greenways Commission and led the effort for public art along the greenways.

Winfield Dunn. Tennessee governor (1971-1975) who oversaw the initial implementation of the Tennessee Natural Areas Preservation Act, including acquisition of Radnor Lake, and supported natural resource conservation statewide.

Jim Forkum. Metro council member representing Madison who consistently supported greenways and expansion of the entire parks system. Instrumental in the acquisition of the Taylor Farm in Neelys Bend to add to Peeler Park.

Richard Fulton. As Nashville's representative in the U.S. Congress, he secured federal funds to help finance the acquisition of Radnor Lake. Then as Nashville's mayor (1975-1988), he was an ardent parks supporter.

Jim Fyke. Served competently as Metro Parks director under several mayors and oversaw the implementation of the greenways program. He then became State Parks director under Gov. Bredesen before being named TDEC commissioner. Restored morale and competence to the State Parks program.

Albert Ganier. Nashville amateur historian and naturalist whose many accomplishments include persuading the L&N Railroad in the 1920s to make Radnor Lake a wildlife sanctuary. Ganier Ridge at Radnor is named for him.

August Gattinger. State geologist in the late 1800s who was the first to recognize the uniqueness of Middle Tennessee's cedar glades.

Bill Haslam. Tennessee governor (2011—) who secured funding for expansion of Radnor Lake. Supported park expansion statewide.

James M. Head. Nashville mayor who appointed the first park board in 1901.

Douglas Henry. A state senator for decades and a tireless champion of conservation. He kept the Harpeth River in Davidson County as a state scenic river and led the successful grass roots fundraising effort to preserve Radnor Lake.

Jesse and Carrie McElyea. Husband and wife, longtime caretakers of Radnor Lake before it came into public ownership.

Bob Miller. State geologist who helped pass the nation's first state scenic river law and who was instrumental in passing the natural areas act that led to saving Radnor Lake.

Jeanie Nelson. Helped start the greenways program under Mayor Bredesen and then became president of The Land Trust for Tennessee.

John Netherton. Nature photographer whose work at Radnor Lake heightened public awareness of the richness of the local landscape.

Phil Ponder. As a member of the Metro Council, he garnered support for the greenways program and was particularly instrumental in developing the Stones River Greenway. Later served as president of Greenways for Nashville.

Mack Prichard. The omnipresent State Parks naturalist whose fingerprints are on every successful conservation effort in Tennessee for a generation. The Godfather of the conservation movement in Tennessee.

Bill Purcell. As Nashville's mayor (1999-2007), he oversaw the development of Beaman and Bells Bend parks, the pedestrian bridge connecting Shelby Bottoms and the Stones River Greenway, and the expansion of nature centers to new parks. An unqualified supporter of parks and greenways.

Elsie Quarterman. The Vanderbilt University botanist made the public aware of the uniqueness of the cedar glades in the Midstate. Her work led to the preservation of many of them, including one in Rutherford County named for her. She was also instrumental in helping preserve Radnor Lake and other Tennessee natural areas.

Lee and Bill Russell. Oak Ridge scientists, husband and wife, and founders of Tennessee Citizens for Wilderness Planning. Moving forces behind most conservation legislation in the 1960-70s, including the scenic rivers act that protects the Harpeth and the natural areas act that protects Radnor Lake.

Tom Shriver. Davidson County's long-time district attorney, later a judge, who was a visible leader in the campaign to save Radnor Lake.

Ronnie Steine. Metro Council member who played a major role in securing initial funding for the Metro Parks greenways.

Ann Tidwell. Served as chair of the Greenways Commission during most of its existence and was president of Greenways for Nashville. Played an indispensable role in getting the greenways program on the ground. Helped develop the Tennessee Scenic Rivers Association and a leader in the ongoing preservation of Radnor Lake.

Charlie Tygard. Metro Council member who sponsored legislation creating the Greenways Commission. A solid greenways advocate.

Percy and Edwin Warner. The visionary brothers who for much of the twentieth century served as chairs of the old Nashville city parks board. They are responsible for the two remarkable parks that bear their names.

Mary Wherry. Metro Parks assistant director who started the first nature center at the Warner Parks.

Kathleen Williams. A pioneer for greenways development in Nashville and statewide through her leadership of the Tennessee Parks and Greenways Foundation.

Oliver Yates. Lipscomb University biologist whose work at Radnor Lake was a major factor in the area being the first area acquired under the natural areas protection law.

APPENDIX THREE

FUTURE OF NASHVILLE'S GREENWAYS AND NATURE PARKS

Nashville's greenways and parks are continually expanding. As this guide was being published, planning and development were in the works for a new greenway in The Gulch, one along the Cumberland River in the Lakewood community between Hermitage and Old Hickory, and extensions of the Mill Creek Greenway in the Cane Ridge community and the Whites Creek Greenway in Bordeaux. Ryman Hospitality Properties, formerly Gaylord Entertainment, has granted Metro Parks an easement for a spur of the Stones River Greenway to reach the Opryland complex. Major new parkland acquisitions are occurring along the Stones River and Whites Creek and at Radnor Lake.

The 2002 Metro Parks master plan calls for adding greenway segments to corridors with existing greenways and adding greenways to the few stream corridors without them. The master plan recommends a larger open space plan, and that was accomplished in 2011.

The Nashville Open Space Plan was sponsored by The Land Trust for Tennessee, completed by the Conservation Fund, and funded by the Martin Foundation. The plan identifies 300 miles of potential greenway trail as well as key undeveloped parcels and offers proposals for conserving them, though not necessarily in public ownership.

At the same time, under the leadership of progressive mayors and governors, Metro Parks and State Parks take advantage of opportunities to acquire land as it becomes available, often from sympathetic owners willing to sell for below market value or, in some cases, donate valuable land. This has occurred at Beaman Park, Peeler Park, Radnor Lake, and the Warner Parks.

Indispensable players in greenway and park expansions are citizen support organizations such as friends groups at Beaman, Radnor, and Warner as well as Greenways for Nashville. They have identified areas for expansion and have taken the lead in acquiring them. The Land Trust for Tennessee plays a key role as well, accepting conservation easements on park expansions to guarantee that they remain open space. (See Appendix Four).

The devastating floods that hit Nashville in May 2010 will result in conversion of some developed areas to green spaces, and it is anticipated that additional parkland will be established along Richland, Whites, and Mill Creeks, and the Cumberland River.

Management agencies are continually updating their websites with the latest information. If you encounter something on the ground that no longer corresponds to what is written in the guide, please email Greenways for Nashville at *www. greenwaysfornashville.org.*

APPENDIX FOUR

SUPPORT ORGANIZATIONS

Conservancy for the Parthenon & Centennial Park. *www.conservancyonline.org*

Cumberland River Compact. *www.cumberlandrivercompact.org*

Friends of Beaman Park. *www.beamanpark.org*

Friends of Bells Bend Park. *www.bellsbend.org*

Friends of Long Hunter State Park. *www.friendsoflonghunter.org*

Friends of Radnor Lake. *www.radnorlake.org*

Friends of Shelby Park & Bottoms. *www.friendsofshelby.org*

Friends of Warner Parks. *www.friendsofwarnerparks.com*

Greenways for Nashville. *www.greenwaysfornashville.org*

Harpeth River Watershed Association. *www.harpethriver.org*

Richland Creek Watershed Alliance.
   www.Richlandcreekwatershedalliance.org

Stones River Watershed Association. *www.stoneswatershed.org*

The Land Trust for Tennessee. *www.landtrusttn.org*

Mayor Karl Dean, left, with the author on the
Richland Creek Greenway

Scale:

0   2 mi

N

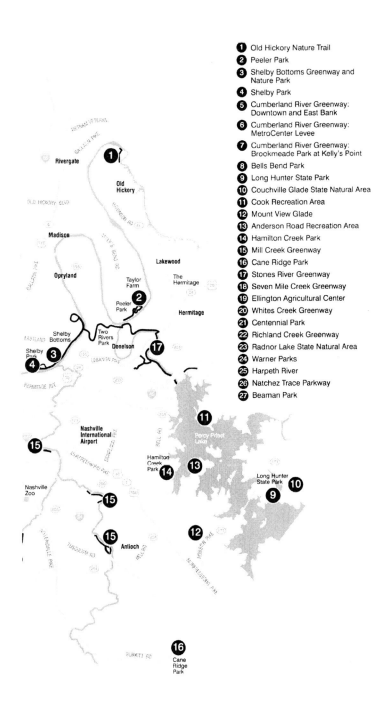

1. Old Hickory Nature Trail
2. Peeler Park
3. Shelby Bottoms Greenway and Nature Park
4. Shelby Park
5. Cumberland River Greenway: Downtown and East Bank
6. Cumberland River Greenway: MetroCenter Levee
7. Cumberland River Greenway: Brookmeade Park at Kelly's Point
8. Bells Bend Park
9. Long Hunter State Park
10. Couchville Glade State Natural Area
11. Cook Recreation Area
12. Mount View Glade
13. Anderson Road Recreation Area
14. Hamilton Creek Park
15. Mill Creek Greenway
16. Cane Ridge Park
17. Stones River Greenway
18. Seven Mile Creek Greenway
19. Ellington Agricultural Center
20. Whites Creek Greenway
21. Centennial Park
22. Richland Creek Greenway
23. Radnor Lake State Natural Area
24. Warner Parks
25. Harpeth River
26. Natchez Trace Parkway
27. Beaman Park

CPSIA information can be obtained at www.ICGtesting.com
Printed in the USA
LVOW06s2222180914

404563LV00009BA/3/P